W9-BNE-440

In**Touch**
with the **W**ord

Lectionary-Based
Prayer Reflections

In Touch with the Word

Lectionary-Based Prayer Reflections

Advent, Christmas, Lent, and Easter

Lisa-Marie Calderone-Stewart

Saint Mary's Press
Christian Brothers Publications
Winona, Minnesota

My thanks go to the following people:
- Mary Parlin and Marilyn Zastrow, for printing these seasonal Scripture reflections in the *West Nebraska Register* before they were ever combined to create this book.
- Bishop Lawrence McNamara, for giving me the opportunity to serve the diocese of Grand Island and for being supportive of me during this project.
- Fr. Bob Stamschror, for your constant affirmation and guidance in this project and in all the projects we envision and accomplish together. It is a joy to work with you.
- Ralph, for the love and care you give me every day, as well as the technical assistance I need whenever our computer doesn't understand what I want it to do.
- Mom, for the enthusiasm you have for my writing and for all of my projects, for all the ideas you give me, and for everything you do for me. I am such a lucky daughter!
- Bishop Ken Untener, you have had a major influence on my spiritual formation, my ministry, and my life.

The publishing team for this book included Robert P. Stamschror, development editor; Laurie Berg Rohda, manuscript editor; Gary J. Boisvert, typesetter; Stephan Nagel and Maurine R. Twait, cover design and art direction; pre-press, printing, and binding by the graphics division of Saint Mary's Press.

The acknowledgments continue on page 204.

Printed in the United States of America

Printing: 9 8 7 6 5 4 3 2 1

Year: 2004 03 02 01 00 99 98 97 96

ISBN 0-88489-399-5, spiral
ISBN 0-88489-375-8, paper

Genuine recycled paper with 10% post-consumer waste. Printed with soy-based ink.

To my parents and godparents, who taught me to pray and share my faith:

To Dad: You listened to my prayers every night at bedtime when I was a child, you listened to my philosophical and theological ramblings when I was writing papers in college, and you are still listening.

To Mom: You never tired of a little girl's conversations about what missionaries do, and if angels still appear, and what heaven is all about, and how to know what God wants us to do; it seems our conversations today aren't all that different.

To Uncle Carl and Aunt Ginny: May I become for my own goddaughter the example of lived faith that you have always been to me.

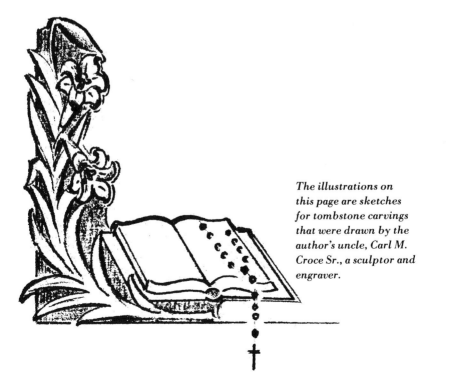

The illustrations on this page are sketches for tombstone carvings that were drawn by the author's uncle, Carl M. Croce Sr., a sculptor and engraver.

Contents

Advent

Christmas Time

Lent

Easter Time

Introduction

Did you ever go to Mass on Sunday, listen to the Scripture readings, and then promptly forget what they were all about or how your life relates to their message? Does this sound familiar? Even though you may have listened to a homilist who connected the word with you and challenged you at that time, what about the week before the Sunday Scriptures or the week after? How can you anticipate and prepare for the word? How can you stay in touch with the word that was heard?

This book is a resource designed to do just that—to help you prepare for the Sunday Scripture readings and to help you stay in touch with the word.

Using This Book

Using *In Touch with the Word* is a simple procedure. First, decide which Sunday's readings you are going to share. If it is Friday afternoon, you might want to reflect on the readings for the next Sunday so you can be more prepared for the upcoming liturgy. If it is Monday morning, you might want to remember the readings you heard on Sunday so you can stay in touch with that word the rest of the week. Next, turn to the page for the Sunday you have in mind. There you will find reflections, questions, and a prayer based on that Sunday's readings.

The Sunday Scripture Readings

The Scripture readings for each Sunday of the year are found in a book called a lectionary. The Sunday readings follow a three-year, A-B-C cycle that continues to repeat itself. The readings in the A cycle highlight the Gospel of Matthew. The readings in the B cycle highlight the Gospel of Mark. The readings in the C cycle highlight the Gospel of Luke. (If you are wondering about the

Gospel of John, don't be concerned. John doesn't really get the short end of the stick! His readings are woven throughout all three years on special days that seem to need that "John" touch.)

The church calendar year consists of the seasons of Advent and Christmas, Lent and Easter, plus Ordinary Time. This book covers the seasons of Advent and Christmas time, Lent and Easter time—the seasons most emphasized in church programs.

Most of the Sundays in these seasons have three sets of readings, one for each cycle. For example, readings are given for the first Sunday of Lent A cycle, the first Sunday of Lent B cycle, and the first Sunday of Lent C cycle. In this case each Sunday also has three sets of reflections, one for each cycle. If you are not sure what cycle the church is in at a given time, the dates for each Sunday cycle are given in the lectionary.

Some dates have only one set of readings—for instance, Christmas and Easter have the same readings for all three cycles—the readings you hear in year A will be the same as those you hear in year B and year C. There is only one set of reflections for those dates as well.

You will note that the Scripture readings are not reprinted in this book. It would make the book too big and too expensive. You will need either a lectionary or a Bible to read one or more of the Scripture readings as part of the prayer reflection. However, a capsulized version of each Scripture reading is provided.

One of the Scripture readings has an open bullet (○) next to it. This indicates which reading will be most focused on in the reflection and which one you might want to read as part of the reflection.

Theme
A summary of a central theme of the readings is also offered. You may want to use it to set a context for the reflection questions that will initiate sharing of and reflecting on the word.

Reflection Questions

The reflection questions for each Sunday address audiences in three categories: adults, teenagers, and children. However, feel free to cross categories in the use of the questions whenever it is appropriate.

Focusing Object

For each set of readings, you will find a suggested focusing object. Using a focusing object in these prayer reflections is not mandatory, but it is helpful, especially with teenagers and children. It is a visual, hands-on reminder of the readings and their message. For example, anticipating or recalling the meaning of the passage about our relationship with Jesus being like a vine and its branches is much easier and more vivid if a plant with a stem and branches is present when reflecting on the reading of that passage.

The focusing object is handy for facilitating the prayer reflection and sharing. For example, after the Scripture reading is proclaimed, the facilitator asks one of the reflection questions for everyone to think about and share their thoughts. Then the facilitator picks up the focusing object and begins the sharing. When finished, the facilitator passes the object to the next person who is ready to share.

The focusing object can be passed around a circle so everyone knows when their turn is coming, or it can be passed randomly as people become ready to share. A large group does better sitting in a circle and passing the object around in order. In a small group—one that fits around a table where everyone can reach the middle—anyone who is ready can pick up the object, share, and replace it for the next person who is ready to take a turn. Also, using the object makes it obvious when a person's turn has ended—no one has to guess. If someone just wants to offer a one-word response, or even remain silent, the focusing object is simply handed to the next person.

The focusing object is more than a reminder or a turn-designator. It is also an effective way to reduce the self-conscious feeling many people get when they are expected to share with a group of their peers. Persons handling an object and looking at it tend to relax and forget that a roomful of people is watching them. People who are relaxed and comfortable do a better job of sharing. This is true of adults, teenagers, and children!

After everyone has had a chance to share, the object comes back to the facilitator who ends with the "Closing" or any other words she or he feels would be appropriate. The focusing object can stay on a kitchen table or a classroom shelf all week, acting as a reminder of God's word and the people's response.

Closing

A closing is provided for each prayer reflection. It consists of a poem or reading that ends the reflections with an inspirational touch. You will notice that the closings come from a variety of cultures and each culture adds a rich spiritual tradition to the prayer reflections.

Indexes

Each Sunday's prayer session is indexed by focusing object and by theme in the back of this book.

Settings

Parish

Parish staffs, councils, and committees usually want to start their meetings with some type of prayer. Prayer based on Sunday's readings is a great way to help the group relate to the parish liturgy, connect with the message of the Sunday readings, and start the meeting off on a spiritual plane.

Homilists can benefit from this resource by looking at the message through the eyes of adults, teenagers, and children. This can provide a springboard for the type of insights needed to be pastoral, effective, and challenging to the assembly of mixed ages that typically gather for Sunday and feast day liturgies. (Actually sharing the reflection questions with adults, teenagers, and children and listening to their responses each week provides even better feedback for a homilist!)

Liturgy planning groups will find this book helpful. Members with different degrees of liturgical experience and understanding can read the theme summaries, share the questions, and get a feel for the flow of the Scriptures. The suggested focusing object can also remind the group to investigate the possibilities of symbolism in the physical environment of the worship space.

Prayer groups and small Christian communities will find *In Touch with the Word* very helpful, especially if the groups include families with children of different ages.

Youth Groupings

Youth ministers will find the prayer reflections in this book a simple way to prepare a youth group or team for the readings they will hear the following Sunday or feast day and to help them stay in touch with the readings they heard the previous Sunday. At the same time, the reflections call attention to the major seasons of the church year. The prayer process in the reflection works equally well with junior high teens or high school teens.

Parish religious education teachers and catechists meeting with a class once a week can use this resource to relate to the Sunday and feast day readings. Sending a note home each week encouraging parents to discuss the readings with their children at the dinner table or at bedtime, perhaps with a similar focusing object, is a good way to weave a family connection into a parish religious education program.

Religion teachers in Catholic schools looking for a way to connect students with their parish community will value this resource. Anticipating or recalling the Scriptures read at the parish liturgies will help students stay in touch with their parish community.

Busy families will find that using *In Touch with the Word* at home is a great way to make liturgical worship more relevant for their teenagers or younger children. Using the prayer reflections does not take long and is easy to do. Best of all, it helps the family as a whole connect with what is said at Mass and remember it throughout the week. Parents may find their teenagers more likely to share prayer if they are doing it "for the sake of their younger brothers and sisters" than if they think they are doing it for themselves!

Parishes with family-based programming can use this resource in several ways. If the parish supplies families with resources to be used at home, every family can receive a copy of *In Touch with the Word* to use on their own. If families gather regularly at the parish for a scheduled activity, the sharing process can be incorporated with the program. If family groups meet in cells or units, they can be provided with copies of this book and suggestions for how it can be used in the context of their meeting.

Whether you work with adults, teenagers, or children in a parish, school, or home setting, you will find that being in touch with the word is easy with *In Touch with the Word.*

Advent

First Sunday of Advent

29 November 1998
2 December 2001
28 November 2004

The Plowshare

Scripture

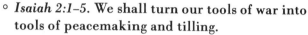

- ○ *Isaiah 2:1–5.* We shall turn our tools of war into tools of peacemaking and tilling.
- *Romans 13:11–14.* Let us cast off deeds of darkness and revel in deeds of light.
- *Matthew 24:37–44.* We must always be ready; we don't know when we will be judged.

Theme

The time is here for us to prepare for the coming of Jesus—for his first coming in Bethlehem and for his final coming at the end of time. Both comings encourage us to reject sin and the ways of darkness, and to embrace goodness and the ways of light. To become ready for the coming of Jesus is to turn our destructive habits into constructive habits.

Focusing Object
A hoe or other gardening tool

Reflections

For Adults

An organization called Swords to Plowshares (P.O. Box 10406, Des Moines, IA 50306) sells plowshare pins. Each pin is a tiny metal replica of a sword that has been twisted into the shape of a plow. It is made from the metal of a scrapped U.S. Air Force F-84 Thunderjet fighter plane, a twentieth-century sword. The card that holds the pin reads, "Waging Peace: Today, there is a deep need for widespread, nonviolent action for peace, because the alternative is unthinkable."

Our world has become so violent that blood and gore entertain us on prime-time television and in movies, and children's handheld video games award points for killing and decapitating the "enemy."

- Do you contribute to the acceptance of violence in today's society? How?
- Do you contribute to the effort of waging peace? How could you do more?
- How is your life different when you take seriously the call to walk in the light and cast off the ways of the darkness?

For Teenagers

Heaven is surely the place without war and tools of destruction. Why can't earth also be such a place? Why can't swords and spears and tools of war and violence be turned into plowshares and pruning hooks and tools for growing things and cultivating life? It would be the best way to get ready for Jesus.

- Name some personality traits that could be thought of as "swords and spears," such as gossiping or using sarcasm and put-downs. Are there "swords and spears" in your personality?
- How can you cultivate spiritual life and growth in your own personality?

The world seems to be getting more violent. Our country has so many murders each day that all of them do not even make the news. Hearing that a human being killed another human being is "no big deal"! We see it all the time on television.

- Why has the world gotten so violent?
- What do you think are the contributing factors to the attitude that violence is an acceptable way to respond to conflict?
- How can a group of young people concerned about violence affect their neighborhood or school?

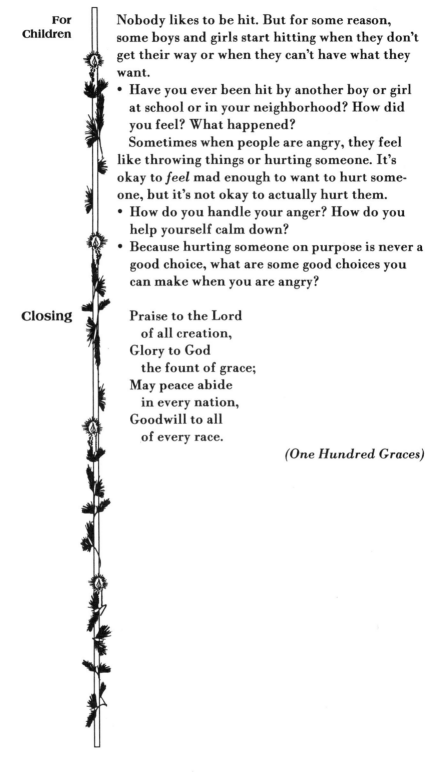

For Children

Nobody likes to be hit. But for some reason, some boys and girls start hitting when they don't get their way or when they can't have what they want.

- Have you ever been hit by another boy or girl at school or in your neighborhood? How did you feel? What happened?

Sometimes when people are angry, they feel like throwing things or hurting someone. It's okay to *feel* mad enough to want to hurt someone, but it's not okay to actually hurt them.

- How do you handle your anger? How do you help yourself calm down?
- Because hurting someone on purpose is never a good choice, what are some good choices you can make when you are angry?

Closing

Praise to the Lord
   of all creation,
Glory to God
   the fount of grace;
May peace abide
   in every nation,
Goodwill to all
   of every race.

(One Hundred Graces)

19

First Sunday of Advent

The Potter and the Clay

Scripture

- ○ *Isaiah 63:16–17; 64:1–8.* God is the potter and we are the clay.
- • *1 Corinthians 1:3–9.* God will sustain us through anything, until the end.
- • *Mark 13:33–37.* We need to be alert and on the watch.

Theme

We need to be alert to God's calling; we need to be watching for what God wants us to do. We need to be clay for our God to shape and mold so that we can be remade, again and again, in God's image. If we are willing to accept God's way, then God will be with us through it all. We will never be alone, and for that we rejoice and are thankful.

Focusing Object
A lump of clay

Reflections

For Adults

The image of God and people as "potter with clay" is not always a popular image. Because the clay has no say in how the potter molds and creates it, the imagery can threaten our free will. The image might work better if seen as a decision on our part, such as, "God, we *choose* to be the clay, and we ask you to be our potter; shape us into what you desire us to be." And once God shapes us, we are still free to choose what we do—we can even choose to reshape ourselves and behave in a manner completely opposite from what God has in mind.

- How does the potter and clay image work for you? Do you welcome being clay? Do you resent or even resist it?
- Recount a time in your life when you invited God to mold you? Was there a time when you shut God out in order to mold yourself?
- How does your life change when you take the following words seriously: "God, you work for those who wait for you"?

For Teenagers

It is hard to be the clay and to let God be the potter. That's like praying, "Whatever you ask of me, God, I'm willing to do it. I'm all yours. Point the way, and I'm walking it."

It is easier to be the potter and want God to be the clay. That's like praying, "God, please do this and do that; please give me this and give me that."

- When did you pray as if you were the potter? What happened? How did you feel?
- Did you ever pray as if you were the clay? If so, what happens? How do you feel? If not, why not? What might happen? And how could you feel?
- What is the hardest challenge God might ask you to accept? What is so hard about it?

For Children

God made all people, animals, and things in the world just as easily as we might make clay people, clay animals, and clay objects. (You might have the children play with clay while they answer these questions.)

- Have you ever played with clay? Do you like to play with clay? What do you enjoy the most about playing with clay?
- Do you think God had fun making us? Why or why not? What sort of things do you think God enjoyed making the most? What animals do you think God liked the best after they were made?

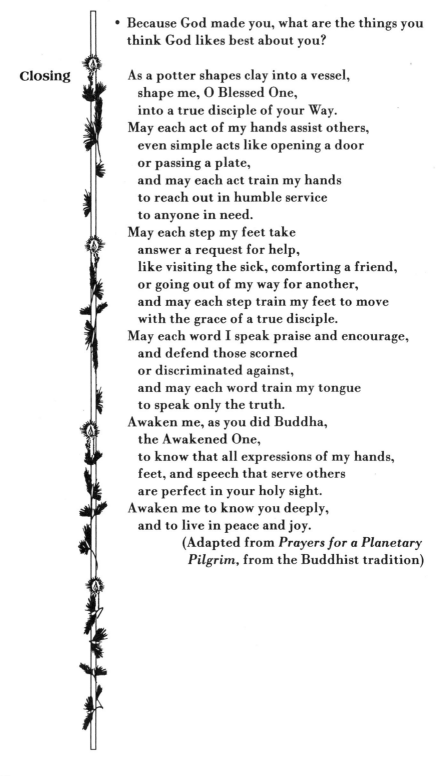

• Because God made you, what are the things you
think God likes best about you?

As a potter shapes clay into a vessel,
   shape me, O Blessed One,
   into a true disciple of your Way.
May each act of my hands assist others,
   even simple acts like opening a door
   or passing a plate,
   and may each act train my hands
   to reach out in humble service
   to anyone in need.
May each step my feet take
   answer a request for help,
   like visiting the sick, comforting a friend,
   or going out of my way for another,
   and may each step train my feet to move
   with the grace of a true disciple.
May each word I speak praise and encourage,
   and defend those scorned
   or discriminated against,
   and may each word train my tongue
   to speak only the truth.
Awaken me, as you did Buddha,
   the Awakened One,
   to know that all expressions of my hands,
   feet, and speech that serve others
   are perfect in your holy sight.
Awaken me to know you deeply,
   and to live in peace and joy.
          (Adapted from *Prayers for a Planetary
          Pilgrim*, from the Buddhist tradition)

First Sunday of Advert

30 November 1997
3 December 2000
30 November 2003

The Branch Springing Forth

Scripture

○ *Jeremiah 33:14–16.* A righteous branch will spring forth from the family of David.
• *1 Thessalonians 3:12—4:2.* May your hearts be filled with innocence and holiness.
• *Luke 21:25–28,34–36.* Watch at all times, and pray that you have strength.

Theme

The branch that springs from David's family tree is Jesus. God's promise made to Israel and Judah is kept when Jesus, the Chosen One, comes. While waiting for Jesus, we need to be watchful, prayerful, and strong. We know that Jesus is our brother and part of our family, and that is enough to fill our hearts with holiness and innocence.

Focusing Object
A branch from a tree or bush

Reflections

For Adults

The family tree theme is important in the Bible. Not only is it mentioned by the prophet Jeremiah, but Isaiah also speaks of "a shoot from the stump of Jesse" (chapter 11). Jesse was David's father, and both the Gospels of Luke (chapter 3) and Matthew (chapter 1) go the distance to show how Jesus is a descendant of Jesse and David.

- Have you ever traced your family tree? Do you know who your ancestors are? Are you aware of the native country or countries of your ancestors? If so, share something about your family heritage and your feelings toward your ancestors. If not, share something you know about your extended family.
- Why is it significant to note that Jesse and David are in Jesus' family tree? Why does it matter to us who a person's relatives are?
- Is it important to know that justice and righteousness are part of your family's history? Why?

For Teenagers

- Have you ever tried to draw your family tree? How many uncles and aunts do you have? How many cousins do you have? How many grandparents do you remember knowing? Are any of them still alive? If so, what are they like? Do you have any older relatives that you really admire? What country or countries are your relatives from?
- Luke and Matthew want us to know that Jesus was born in King David's family. How would you feel if you found out that one of your ancestors was a king or queen?
- What do you think your children and grandchildren might be like? Where do you think they might live? What country do you hope they will live in? What do you hope for all people living in the world by the time your children or grandchildren are grown?

For Children

Note: If sharing these questions with your family, you could hang small pictures of your extended family from different parts of the tree branch.

In a family, people are related to one another in different ways. Two people could be mother and son, brother and sister, grandfather and granddaughter, and so on. When you draw a picture of your family, with lines to show how everyone is related to one another, it is called a "family tree."

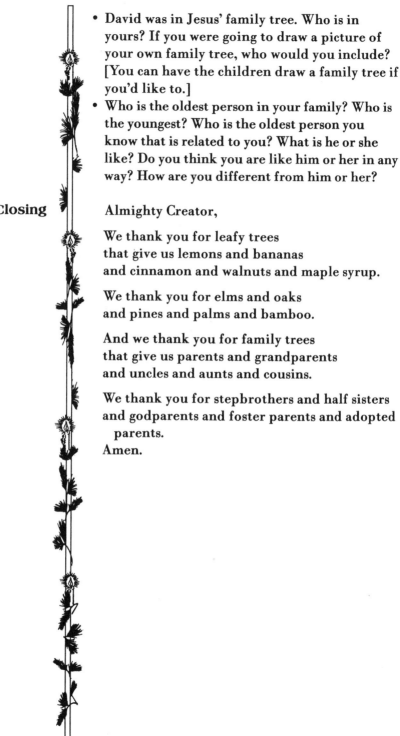

- David was in Jesus' family tree. Who is in yours? If you were going to draw a picture of your own family tree, who would you include? [You can have the children draw a family tree if you'd like to.]
- Who is the oldest person in your family? Who is the youngest? Who is the oldest person you know that is related to you? What is he or she like? Do you think you are like him or her in any way? How are you different from him or her?

Closing

Almighty Creator,

We thank you for leafy trees
that give us lemons and bananas
and cinnamon and walnuts and maple syrup.

We thank you for elms and oaks
and pines and palms and bamboo.

And we thank you for family trees
that give us parents and grandparents
and uncles and aunts and cousins.

We thank you for stepbrothers and half sisters
and godparents and foster parents and adopted
  parents.
Amen.

Second Sunday of Advent

6 December 1998
9 December 2001
5 December 2004

The Animal Kingdom

Scripture

○ *Isaiah 11:1–10.* The wolf, lamb, leopard, snake, and child can all be together at peace.
• *Romans 15:4–9.* Live in harmony and be welcoming to each other.
• *Matthew 3:1–12.* John the Baptizer in the wilderness tells us, "Prepare the way."

Theme

The time will come when truth and justice will reign over wickedness. Even in the animal kingdom there will be peace, with no animal trying to kill another. John the Baptizer tells us to repent and to prepare the way for God, and that means changing disharmony to harmony and hostility to acceptance.

Focusing Object
A set of plastic animals or a picture of different animals together

Reflections

For Adults

Sometimes it is easier to love the world than to love our neighbor whose trash keeps blowing onto our driveway and whose dog keeps doing its business on our lawn. Sometimes a relationship with a spouse, coworker, roommate, or sibling can be as antagonistic as a relationship between rival animals.

- Who is the most difficult person for you to make peace with? Who is the one that is hardest to forgive?
- Whose point of view is most difficult for you to welcome and understand? What can you do about it?
- Do you consider yourself meek? Have you been taken advantage of by others? Have you ever taken advantage of others?
- How is your life different when you take seriously the message that the meek of the earth will receive their due and the wicked will be laid low?

For Teenagers

Human beings are supposed to be more "civilized" than animals. We have jobs. We have hobbies. We celebrate holidays. Yet we can learn from animals. When we see a pride of lions stalking a cape buffalo on television, we don't think badly of the lions—lions are supposed to hunt and kill. It is in their nature. But what about people? The pride of people can also kill, even when stomachs aren't empty. You won't see lions doing that.

- What can we "civilized" people learn from the animal kingdom?
- If you were an ambassador for the United Nations, what would you do in order to stop countries from fighting? How would you prevent one people's pride from causing the killing of other people? How would you encourage world peace? What plans would you present?

For Children

- Why isn't there just one cage at the zoo? Why do all the different animals need separate cages? What would happen if they were all in the same cage?
- Some animals are safer to play with than others. Which animals are safe to play with? Which animals are unsafe to play with?

- What would it be like if all the animals in the whole world became safe playmates for all children? Which animals would you want to ride? Which animal would you want for a pet? Which animal would you want living in your house?

Closing

Earlier this year, a baby was born in Old Blue,
      miles from nowhere.
In December, I saw a pride of lions downing
and devouring
      a huge cape-buffalo bull.
In January, there was a spitting cobra in our
store-room—
      four-feet long,
      hood-flared,
      cornered,
      so close, it spit on Nyangaka.
In February, I received a gift of a lamb from
Nahuchu
for helping to join the healthy of Nebraska
with the
      sick of the Serengeti.
  The lion,
  The lamb,
  The viper,
  The child.
    Before all prophets,
    before us, lions do roar,
      lambs are silent,
      vipers evoke fear,
      babies inspire peace.
Inside us,
  Africa,
  the uni-verse, lions,
    lambs,
    vipers,
    children live the paradox of sad-delight
    under the shade of the divine acacia.
                ("Under the Acacia Tree")

Second Sunday of Advent

8 December 1996
5 December 1999
8 December 2002

Be Comforted

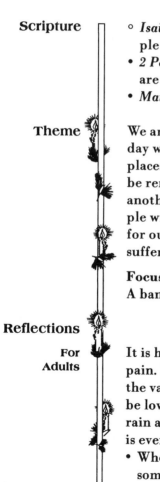

Scripture

○ *Isaiah 40:1–5,9–11*. Comfort, comfort, my people . . . speak tenderly.
• *2 Peter 3:8–14*. One day and a thousand years are the same with God.
• *Mark 1:1–8*. Prepare the way of our God.

Theme

We are to be comforted by the promise that the day will come when valleys, hills, and hiding places that separate and divide humankind will be removed, and we will live in unity with one another and God. We are called to comfort people with this hope, and to help prepare this way for our God even in the midst of the pain and suffering that is still with us.

Focusing Object
A bandage or Band-Aid

Reflections

For Adults

It is hard to wait for comfort when we are in pain. It is not easy to believe the promise that the valleys will be raised and the mountains will be lowered when we are looking at bumpy terrain ahead and are not up for the suffering. Who is ever up for suffering anyway?
• When did you truly receive comfort? How was someone really present to your needs and how did they make a difference in your suffering?

• How would your life be different if you took more seriously the message to be of comfort to God's people?

Waiting for Christmas is hard. It is hard to wait for anything. But it is especially frustrating to wait for something when you don't know how long it will take or what is holding it up—for example, driving along on a busy highway and coming upon a traffic jam that cannot be explained. As far as you can see there is no accident, no construction, no reason for all four lanes to be at a standstill. But if you have been in such a situation long enough, you have seen what almost always happens. Sooner or later people start trickling out of their cars to talk to one another. They start sharing food, telling stories, getting acquainted, and cracking jokes. Suddenly the waiting doesn't seem like such torture. Why? Because people begin to comfort one another. And who usually starts it? Young people!

• How does attitude affect waiting and even pain? How does comfort affect attitude?
• When have you been comforted by a friend or a family member? What words helped? What actions helped? What did he or she try to do for you? Have you ever been able to be of comfort to another? What have you done or said? What happened?

• Have you ever needed a bandage? What happened? Did anyone help you? What did they do?
• Which would you like better when you hurt yourself: to have someone there helping you, asking you if you are all right, and putting a bandage on? or to be all alone and have no one even know that you are bleeding? Even if you know where the Band-Aids are and how to put them on, isn't it nice to have someone there anyway? Why or why not?

Closing

Come, Lord Jesus!
I open my mind and heart and soul,
And long for You to be born anew in me.
Help me to experience Your presence within me,
And to allow You to touch the earth through me.

Come, Lord Jesus!
Come and stay with my family and friends—
And all who are dear to me. Be near
Especially those who are burdened by
sickness or sadness—set them free
By your love and care.

Come, Lord Jesus!
Bring peace to our world. May we hear again
Your own prayer: "That we may be one."
And may we learn anew to follow your example:
"That there may be bread" for all.

We hunger, we thirst, we wait for you!
Come, Lord Jesus!
And do not delay!

(One Hundred Graces)

Second Sunday of Advent

7 December 1997
10 December 2000
7 December 2003

Thankfulness for Partnership

Scripture

- *Baruch 5:1–9.* We will be led with joy in the light of God's glory.
- *Philippians 1:4–6,8–11.* I am thankful for your partnership in the Gospel.
- *Luke 3:1–6.* All people shall see salvation from God.

Theme

Saint Paul is beside himself with joy and thankfulness for the partnership of the wonderful people who help him spread the good news of the Gospel message. Such people as Saint Paul are filled with joy and light; they are aware of the gift of salvation from our God. Such people will affect the world with peace and joy, beauty and justice.

Focusing Object
A thank-you note

Reflections

For Adults

- Think about one of your best accomplishments. Did you succeed alone or did you have a partner who helped? Was this person a partner only for this particular accomplishment or for many things?

- Do you have a best friend—a friend who truly has been a partner in life? Describe this person, how you met, and how your life has been enriched by this partnership.
- God promises that every good work we do will be brought to completion at the day of Jesus Christ. How would human life be changed if this promise were taken seriously?

For Teenagers

Saint Paul is so thankful for his friends who are his "partners" in spreading the Gospel.

- Who are your partners in life? Do you have a best friend or a group of friends that partner you and one another through life's ups and downs? Describe such a friend. Are you thankful for this special friendship? How do you show your thankfulness?
- Are you a thankful person in general? Do you write a lot of thank-you notes? Do you always remember to say thank you when you are given something? Do you often consider all the things you have to be thankful for? How can you improve in this area?
- What do you think it means to be a partner in spreading the Gospel? What would Gospel-spreading partners do?

For Children

- Who are the special people in your life who love you? What kind of things do they do for you? Do you ever thank them for all their love and help? How do you thank them?
- Do you have a best friend? What is that person like? What makes this person your best friend? Have you ever told this person thank you for being your best friend?
- Jesus had some best friends. They were his partners in trying to make the world a better place. If Jesus walked into your room today and asked you to be his partner and help him make the world a better place, would you say yes? What kind of things would you do for your partner Jesus?

Closing

The job of the Peacemaker is
to stop war
to purify the world
to get it saved from poverty and riches
to heal the sick
to comfort the sad
to wake up those who have not yet found God
to create joy and beauty wherever you go
to find God in everything and in everyone.
(Muriel Lester, from a Fellowship of
Reconciliation bookmark)

Third Sunday of Advent

Flowers

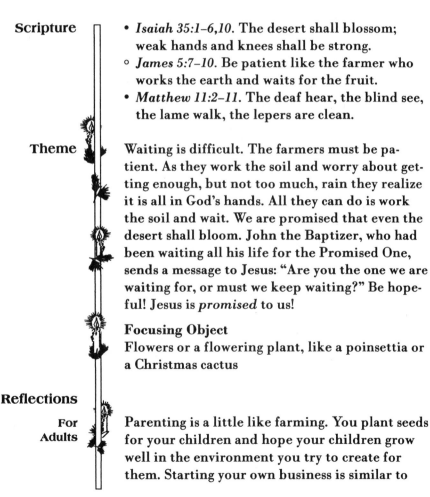

Scripture

- *Isaiah 35:1–6,10.* The desert shall blossom; weak hands and knees shall be strong.
- *James 5:7–10.* Be patient like the farmer who works the earth and waits for the fruit.
- *Matthew 11:2–11.* The deaf hear, the blind see, the lame walk, the lepers are clean.

Theme

Waiting is difficult. The farmers must be patient. As they work the soil and worry about getting enough, but not too much, rain they realize it is all in God's hands. All they can do is work the soil and wait. We are promised that even the desert shall bloom. John the Baptizer, who had been waiting all his life for the Promised One, sends a message to Jesus: "Are you the one we are waiting for, or must we keep waiting?" Be hopeful! Jesus is *promised* to us!

Focusing Object
Flowers or a flowering plant, like a poinsettia or a Christmas cactus

Reflections

For Adults

Parenting is a little like farming. You plant seeds for your children and hope your children grow well in the environment you try to create for them. Starting your own business is similar to parenting also. They both take patience and hope.

- Did you ever plant a garden as a child? as an adult? What was it like the first time anything began to grow? What was it like the first time you tasted one of your own vegetables or smelled one of your own flowers? Before the first signs of growth appeared, were you hopeful? When the rain didn't come, were you patient? Do you remember thinking, "Nothing is ever going to grow here"? Why or why not?
- Share a story about a time in your life when hope and patience were very hard to come by.

For Teenagers

More than any other season of the year, the weeks before Christmas are a time when young people learn patience and hope. Imaginations run wild with visions of vacation time and presents, and the weeks seem to take forever.

- Who is the most patient and hopeful person you know? What is she or he like? How does her or his patience and sense of hope affect others? How can you try to be like that person?
- What is something you are hoping for? What is something you are expecting, something that makes it hard to be patient?

For Children

- Did you ever plant any seeds? Do you know anyone who did? What happened? What would happen to seeds if you planted them and then, when they sprouted, you covered the plants up so they wouldn't get any sun or water? Would they grow? Why not?
- Is it hard to wait for seeds to grow? Why? Is it hard to wait for Christmas to come? Why? Which is harder—waiting for seeds to grow or waiting for Christmas to come? Why?

Closing

Come gentle rain of Advent-tide,
    soak deep into my heart,
    calling forth signs of an early spring.
Make buds appear on my heart's barren
        rosebush
    and blooms on its dried flower stalks.

Come showers of silence and wet my soul;
    soak deeply with your fertile fingers,
    dripping heaven's dew.
May I come forth from my times of prayer
    as from a bath:
    dripping wet from a sacred soaking,
    refreshed, renewed, revitalized.

Advent prayer of December stillness,
    dampen my dry soul,
    coax forth green leaves of the Spirit
    and bring forth buds of bright flowers
    as green trees flicker with magic lights
    and green wreath circles
    whirl on front doors,
    red-bowed in festive joy.

. . . .

Radiant Rain God,
    make me your brimful cloud,
    ready to shower down Emmanuel's justice
        and peace
    upon all I meet.

(Prayers for a Planetary Pilgrim)

Third Sunday of Advent

15 December 1996
12 December 1999
15 December 2002

A Year of Favor

Scripture

- ○ *Isaiah 61:1–2,10–11.* Good tidings! The year of favor.
- • *1 Thessalonians 5:16–24.* Rejoice, pray, give thanks.
- • *John 1:6–8,19–28.* John came to bear witness to the light.

Theme

In Isaiah's time, every seventh year was a year of favor during which all debts were canceled and captives were released. The year of favor reflected the mercy and forgiveness of God. The time of the coming of Jesus as the Messiah is also a year of favor, likewise bringing God's mercy and forgiveness. The First Letter to the Thessalonians tells us to rejoice, pray, and give thanks constantly—a fitting response to the goodness of God, and to God's mercy and forgiveness in the coming of Jesus.

Focusing Object
A calendar

Reflections

For Adults

The passage in Isaiah about the year of favor is what Jesus chose to read in the synagogue in Nazareth. He returned there shortly after he began his public ministry. He said to those present in the synagogue that the passage in the Scriptures was fulfilled in their hearing of it. If the "year of favor" is the year of Jesus, then every year is a year of favor if we make Jesus the center of our life.

- What would be a year of favor for you? From what would you like to be freed? For what mourning would you like to be comforted? From which barren ground would you like to see a garden spring up?
- How could the situation of our global human family change if we took having a year of favor seriously?

For Teenagers

You have probably heard of political prisoners being captured and released. In your local newspapers, you have probably seen pictures of men and women getting married. You have probably seen gardens all over your town. This sounds like the year of favor that Isaiah was talking about.

- Do you think it is? Why or why not?
- Are there plenty of things to be thankful for and to rejoice about? Name some.

When Jesus came, he fulfilled these Scriptures of Isaiah. Jesus comes for us again and again every year at Christmas time. During Advent we do our best to prepare for Jesus in our hearts—to get ourselves ready to help Jesus make this year a year of favor.

- How can you help make this a year of favor in your school? in your neighborhood? in your family?

For Children

Jesus says that every year with him is a year of favor, a special year. When Jesus was teaching his disciples how to live, he did some special things, like healing the blind so they could see, healing the deaf so they could hear, and healing the lame so they could walk. He made poor people, old people, and sad people feel wonderful, simply because he was with them. He cared about them and helped them.

• If Jesus came into your house to make this year a special year, what would you ask Jesus to do?

Just as Jesus taught his disciples to help others, the church teaches us to help others. When people are busy helping other people, everyone has a special year of favor.

• Do you know anyone who does a lot of helping? Who do they help? What do they do for other people? How do they help make every year a year of favor?

Closing

When you arise in the morning, give
thanks for the morning light. Give
thanks for your life and your strength.
Give thanks for your food and give
thanks for the joy of living. And
if you see no reason for giving thanks,
rest assured the fault is in yourself.

(*American Indian Prayers and Poetry*,
a prayer from the Sioux Indian tradition)

Third Sunday of Advent

REJOICE IN THE LORD

Rejoice for the Almighty!

Scripture

- *Zephaniah 3:14–18.* Almighty God will rejoice with love for you!
- *Philippians 4:4–7.* Rejoice! Your Almighty Redeemer is here!
- *Luke 3:10–18.* I'm not worthy to untie the sandal of the Almighty One.

Theme

Rejoice! Rejoice! Advent is more than half over! It will be Christmas soon! And the Mighty One is coming! How mighty is this Mighty One? So mighty that even John the Baptizer, one of the holiest men to ever live, was not worthy enough to untie the Mighty One's sandal! Who is this Mighty One? Jesus! The Almighty One who arrived as a helpless infant!

Focusing Object
A shoe or sandal with strings or straps that can be unfastened

Reflections

For Adults

Great joy always fills the house when a loved one is coming to visit. Special food is prepared, homes are cleaned and decorated, activities are planned, and the spirit of joyful anticipation overrides everything else. That is essentially the spirit of Advent—getting ready for Christmas, for Jesus, and for all who will come.

- Share a story about this type of joyful anticipation in your life.
- What does it mean to be unworthy to untie some mighty person's sandal strap? How might life be different if God's mighty power was taken more seriously?

For Teenagers

In the days of John the Baptizer, untying a sandal strap was the work of a slave. People's feet got mighty dirty every day from walking along the dusty roads. When you entered the home of a person who was rich enough to own a slave, the slave would untie your sandals and wash your feet. Imagine a person so mighty, that even John the Baptizer was unworthy to untie his sandals.

- Have you ever felt unworthy? Did you ever meet someone you were in awe of? Did you ever receive an honor you felt you hardly deserved? If so, talk about what it was like. If not, can you imagine it? Who would be the person, and what would be the situation that could make you feel unworthy?

The third Sunday of Advent is meant to be a day of awesome, incredible, totally magnificent joy. Rejoice is a key word and concept in the readings.

- Has anything ever brought you awesome, incredible, totally magnificent joy? Describe what that sort of joy might be for you.
- Jesus—the Messiah, the Almighty One, the Chosen One of God, the Savior of the Universe— is coming. Does his coming seem to bring on a joy that is awesome, incredible, and totally magnificent?
- Do Christmas and even Jesus seem overrated in this world? Why or why not?

For Children

- John the Baptizer was trying to explain to us how mighty and wonderful Jesus is. Who is the most wonderful person you know? What would be the most wonderful thing you could ever do? Is it hard to imagine Jesus doing something even more wonderful than that?

- Christmas is coming, and today is a good day to get excited about Christmas. What makes Christmas exciting? What are you looking forward to the most?

- Christmas is a celebration of Jesus' birthday. But sometimes, when people get excited about Christmas, they forget about Jesus. How can you help yourself and your family remember that Jesus is the reason for celebrating Christmas?

Closing

May the blessing of God rest upon you,
May the peace of God abide with you,
May the presence of God illuminate your heart
Now and forever.

          (*One Hundred Graces*, a Sufi blessing)

Fourth Sunday of Advent

20 December 1998
23 December 2001
19 December 2004

Dreaming and Waking

Scripture

- *Isaiah 7:10–14.* We are told a woman shall conceive and give birth to a son, Emmanuel.
- *Romans 1:1–7.* The prophets promised us the Chosen One of the Gospels.
- *Matthew 1:18–24.* A dream tells Joseph to wed Mary; he awakens and goes to her.

Theme

Joseph was troubled because his wife-to-be was pregnant. He went to sleep thinking that he might not marry her, when a dream assured him that Mary's pregnancy was from the Holy Spirit and that her son would be the Savior. He went to sleep upset, but because of his dream, he awoke resolved and committed. The son of the woman he loved would be the Chosen One Joseph had learned about from studying the prophets.

Focusing Object
A pillow

Reflections

For Adults

Many times we go to sleep troubled, and during the night our rest and the passing of time help us sort out our thoughts so we are more resolved in the morning. Things often look overwhelming at night, yet by morning a fresh perspective helps us cope and make a decision.

- When was a time that you had a difficult decision to make, and "sleeping on it" helped you find the right thing to do?

Joseph had an enormous burden and responsibility. In order for him to believe that Mary was truly pregnant by the Holy Spirit, he had to fully embrace the notion that this son was the Messiah that he had prayed for his whole life. Not his own flesh and blood, but more than that! The flesh and blood of humanity, for humanity. And he was to help Mary raise this Messiah. Obviously, he was not expecting this!

- Were you ever suddenly given a huge responsibility that you were not expecting? Was it something that pleased you and scared you at the same time?

For Teenagers

You might never have thought about this, but Mary, the mother of Jesus, was a pregnant, unwed teenager. The man she was to marry knew that he was not the father of her child. It is an astonishing story—astonishing because it happened and because Joseph came to believe it.

- How would most of your male friends respond in this situation? What would most of your female friends say if they heard Mary's story about the Holy Spirit?
- What is the most astonishing story anyone ever told you? Did you believe them? Why or why not? Do you have a friend who is so close to you that you would believe anything he or she told you—even a story as astonishing as Mary's?

Joseph did not believe Mary at first. A message from a dream helped him believe. Dreams can be powerful.

- Do you remember your dreams? Do you dream in color? Have you ever tried to keep a notebook by your bed and write a dream journal? Have you ever had a dream that calmed you and helped you make a decision or deal with a difficult situation? Have your dreams ever affected the way you felt when you woke up?

Joseph had a dream from God that helped him
understand that Mary was supposed to be his
wife and that her baby would be Jesus.
* Do you ever have dreams about people you
  know? Can you remember any of your dreams?
  Joseph went to bed upset and unhappy, but
when he woke up, he felt better.
* Do you remember a time when you went to bed
  upset or unhappy or not feeling good, but then
  you woke up feeling better? What happened?

Closing

Almight Creator of the Sun,

Thank you for mornings!

Thank you for sleepy visions
    through half-shut eyelids
    that stir us from our dreams.

Thank you for yawning
    with eyes shut tight
    and mouth open wide like a lion
    in the middle of a roar.

Thank you for stretching
    for arms and legs and fingers and toes
    that reach and reach until they creak with
        delight.

Thank you for sunrises
    and new beginnings
    that remind us the dark night is over;
    that greet us with another glorious day,
    a new creation,
    one more opportunity to wake up and to
        serve you well.

Amen.

Fourth Sunday of Advent

The Angel

Scripture

• *2 Samuel 7:1–5,8–11,16.* David's house and lineage will be great.
• *Romans 16:25–27.* To God be glory forever!
○ *Luke 1:26–38.* The angel Gabriel visits Mary.

Theme

Gabriel visits Mary and her life is changed forever. She agrees to be the mother of the Savior of the world, and her son is to be born in the house and lineage of David. This miracle is just the beginning of many more to come—and all miracles give glory to God.

Focusing Object
An angel

Reflections

For Adults

In the Scriptures, angels are messengers and heralds and guides. Sometimes they have names, other times they do not.
• What was your childhood understanding of angels? How is it different from your current understanding?
In this story from Luke, Gabriel is a herald who declares that Mary is a highly favored daughter, and explains the divine plan of her son's birth. Gabriel is also a guide who calms Mary and tells her not to be afraid.

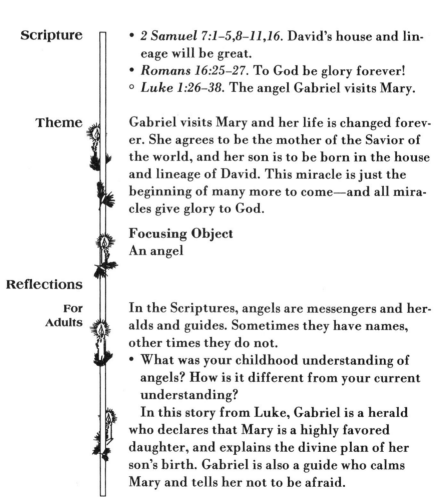

• Who has been a guide in your life? Who has taken the role of messenger or herald of God in your life?

For Teenagers

Lots of paintings, movies, and TV specials have shown Gabriel visiting Mary. Usually, it is dramatic and fascinating.

• How do you think the visitation really happened? Do you think Gabriel flew through the window or just appeared out of thin air? Do you think Gabriel was really there or is the angel just a literary symbol? How else could Mary have received her message? What do you suppose Mary was thinking?

Angels are popular decorations, and they appear as characters in TV programs, movies, and stories. Their appeal has increased recently.

• Why do you think people are so interested in angels? Do you believe in angels? Do you believe you have your own guardian angel? If not, why not? If so, what do you think your guardian angel does?

• What do you think the purpose of angels is? What can angels do that people cannot? Do you think you can communicate with angels? Why or why not?

For Children

• The Bible tells us that an angel came to visit Mary. What would you do if an angel came to visit you? What would you say? What would a visit from an angel be like?

• Do you think God still sends angels with special messages to people?

• Do you think your guardian angel watches over you? If so, what do you think your guardian angel looks like?

Closing

Angel of God,
My Guardian dear,
To whom God's love
Entrusts me here.
Ever this day
Be at my side
To light and guard,
To rule and guide.
Amen.

(A form of the traditional
"Prayer to My Guardian Angel")

Fourth Sunday of Advent

21 December 1997
24 December 2000
21 December 2003

Blessed
Is the Fruit
of Your Womb

Scripture

- *Micah 5:2–4.* From Bethlehem shall be born the Most High.
- *Hebrews 10:5–10.* Jesus comes to do the will of God.
- *Luke 1:39–45.* Elizabeth greets Mary, both are pregnant, both are filled with joy.

Theme

In the tiny town of Bethlehem the savior of all humanity is to be born—a tiny helpless infant. This infant appears just like any other—a blessing to a mother, a joy to other members of the family, and a miracle. When Elizabeth greets Mary, her joy is so complete that even Elizabeth's own baby feels it. This instance of cousin meeting cousin, pregnant woman meeting pregnant woman, represents the will of God in the flesh.

Focusing Object
A baby rattle, baby quilt, baby shoes, or the like

Reflections

**For
Adults**

A pregnant woman is a miracle. You or your spouse may have given birth. If not, perhaps your sister or a close friend has. You may have actually witnessed a baby being born. Maybe you are close to someone who has miscarried, who has had an abortion, or whose baby died before, during, or shortly after childbirth.

- What is your experience with pregnancy? with birth? Whatever your experience, share some of the feelings you have about pregnancy and the birth of a baby.
- The Scriptures tell us that those who believe in the word of God will be fulfilled. How is life changed when you take this message seriously?

For Teenagers

When Elizabeth and Mary met, they were both pregnant, and they were both filled with joy and hope. But sometimes when a woman finds she is pregnant, it isn't always good news. Sometimes it takes quite an adjustment, and sometimes difficult decisions must be made.

- Do you know anyone who has been pregnant? Do you know what kind of an experience it was for her? What do you see as the joys and the challenges of being pregnant?
- Have you ever played with a baby? Have you ever held a newborn? Have you ever changed a baby's diaper? Have you ever fed a baby? How much time have you spent with babies? How do you feel about babies?

For Children

Elizabeth was Mary's cousin. Elizabeth was going to have a baby named John. Mary was going to have a baby named Jesus.

- Have you ever held a baby? How big was the baby? What did the baby do? Do babies need a lot of help? Why? What do they need help with?

Elizabeth and Mary were both very happy to be having babies. They had to wait a long time for their babies to be born. Waiting for Jesus to come at Christmas is a little like Mary waiting for Jesus to be born.

- When you were born, lots of people were probably waiting for you. Do you know any stories about yourself as a baby? What season were you born in? Can you guess what the weather was like?

51

Closing

O Creator of all Life,
  We ask you to bless all your daughters
  Who have been given the marvelous gift
  of life to bear within their bodies.
We rejoice as did Elizabeth and Mary,
  and we pray that these precious children,
  alive within their mothers,
  may soon join us in the light of day.
May Mary and Elizabeth
  and all the Holy Women and
  Heavenly Mothers of past ages
  be with your daughters
  as they await childbirth.
May their strength help these earthly mothers
  carry their babies,
  so that when that hour,
  hidden from the beginning of time,
  finally arrives,
  their children of God may come forth
  into the world
  wrapped with love, joy, and peace.
May the blessing of God, Compassionate as a
    Mother,
  of God the Son, and of God the Holy Spirit
  rest upon all pregnant women
  and their yet unborn babies.
Amen.
  (Adapted from "Blessing Prayer for a Mother
                              with Child")

Christmas Time

Midnight Mass

*25 December
every year*

𝒜 Child Is
Born to Us

Scripture

- *Isaiah 9:2–7.* A child is born to us: Wonderful, Counselor, Almighty God!
- *Titus 2:11–14.* Live sincere, upright, and godly lives, awaiting your blessed hope, Jesus!
- *Luke 2:1–14.* The babe was wrapped in swaddling clothes, lying in a manger.

Theme

The prophet proclaims a Wonder Person to come! A Counselor, an Everlasting Holy One, the Bringer of Peace! We are told to live upright and godly lives as we await our blessed hope, the Messiah, our Savior! How does he arrive? In a golden chariot, upon the clouds with a blast of trumpets? No, he comes as a baby, born in a cave, the newest member of a homeless family. He sleeps in the straw.

Focusing Object
A handful of straw

Reflections

**For
Adults**

There is something outrageous—preposterous—about the Savior of the Universe, the Messiah of Eternity, the baby of Almighty God, who is Almighty God, being born in the side of a hill, in a makeshift stable, because all the inns in Bethlehem were filled and Mary and Joseph did not have a reservation. The queen of England would never have a child in such conditions. Neither would the president of the United States. Nor would they need a reservation for the most suitable birthing place possible. So why would God? Why would God choose an unwed teenager in the first place? And a stepfather who does not have the clout to get an appropriate room for his wife to give birth in.

- Why might God choose such a poor environment for such a blessing? What are we called upon to learn from this story? Why might you choose the poor to do great things? What are some ways you can be blessed by the poor?

Jesus was laid in a manger, a feeding trough. Jesus, who was to become our bread and wine, our food, was laid to sleep on the animals' dinner table.

- In what way is Jesus your nourishment? In what way does Jesus feed you?

For Teenagers

For people surrounded by department store decorations, commercials, Christmas carols, special foods, and the like, believing that today's Christmas celebration actually evolved from the humble story of a young woman giving birth in the straw is a stretch. It might help to focus on the characters involved.

- What do you think went through Joseph's mind as he witnessed Mary giving birth to a baby? What do you think went through Mary's mind as she struggled with the birth experience?

The Christmas story is full of symbols. Jesus, who becomes our bread and wine—our nourishment—is laid in a manger, the feeding trough for the animals. Jesus, who is the champion of poor people, is born into a homeless family. Poor shepherds were the first to welcome the Messiah that the Jewish people had been awaiting for generations. The symbol of angels singing, praising God, and flying madly all over the sky was a good clue that something out of the ordinary was happening.

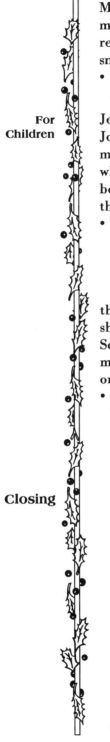

Modern Christmas stories use different symbols to make the same points: Rudolph, the "poorest" reindeer, becomes the champion; and Frosty, a snowman, transforms children's lives.

- What story from your own personal Christmas experiences has special meaning or symbolism?

For Children

Jesus was born in the straw because Mary and Joseph were in a stable, and straw is what the animals slept on. Poor children around the world who do not own beds might also sleep on straw because it can be piled up high, making it softer than the ground. But straw can also feel scratchy.

- Have you ever slept on straw? Have you ever seen animals resting on straw in a zoo or at a farm? Would you rather sleep in a bed with a mattress or on a pile of straw? Why?

Many families have a little manger scene in their home with Jesus, Mary, and Joseph, some sheep and cows, shepherds, and some straw. Some people say that every piece of straw in that manger scene represents a good deed that someone in that house did for someone else.

- Do you have a manger scene in your house? Where? If it has straw, how many pieces of straw do you think there are? What are some good deeds that you do, or can do, to help someone else?

Closing

Señora doña María,
I come from far away
And I bring a pair of rabbits
to the little Child today.

Squash, I bring, potatoes,
and flour for poor Ana.
Mamma, Pappa send regards;
so does old Aunt Juana.

In the crèche of Bethlehem
are sun, moon, stars galore,
The Virgin and St. Joseph
and Jesus in the straw.

(*Peace on Earth*, a traditional poem from Chile)

Feast
of the Holy Family

The Family

Scripture

Note: The first two readings are the same for all three cycles of the Feast of the Holy Family. The Gospel reading changes for each cycle.

• *Sirach 3:2–6,12–14.* Children are asked to love and bring honor to their parents.
• *Colossians 3:12–21.* Husbands, wives, children, and parents: Love one another.
◦ *Matthew 2:13–15,19–23.* Joseph is given messages in dreams.

Theme

Families are so different. Many families have a mother and a father living together with children. Some families have children living with a mother; some have children living with a father. In other families, stepsisters and stepbrothers and half sisters and half brothers live together. Some families have no sisters or brothers at all. Some families have a husband and wife, and no children. Some families have grandparents living with their grandchildren. Some have uncles or aunts or nieces or nephews living with them. Some families have one single person living alone in the house. Some families are made up of two people that are really good friends and enjoy being roommates. But the one thing all good families have in common is love.

Focusing Object
A picture of your family

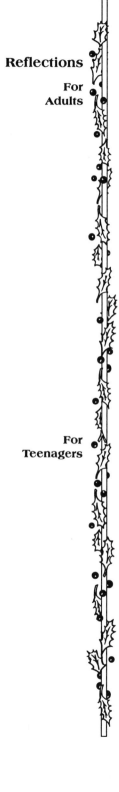

Reflections

For Adults

Joseph clearly loved his family. He received a message from God in a dream that his child's life was in danger. He got up and was ready to go in the middle of the night.

- What helpful things do you remember your mother or father (or older relative or guardian) doing for you when you were a child? Were you ever sick in the middle of the night? Did you ever have a difficult journey? If you are a parent, what have you had to do for your children? What unexpected surprises have come with parenting?

- Joseph and Mary had to suddenly move their family to Egypt, without warning, and in the middle of the night. Have you ever had to make a decision to move abruptly? If so, how many people were affected by that decision? What was it like? If not, what do you think would be the most difficult part of having to move?

For Teenagers

Imagine being Mary when Joseph awakens her in the middle of the night to tell her that he had a dream from God and they need to move the whole family to Egypt right away because the baby's life is in danger.

- What do you think they packed? What would you pack if you were suddenly awakened and had to move immediately? What would you be thinking?

- A parent makes all kinds of sacrifices for his or her children. What is one sacrifice you can think of that a parent made for you? What sacrifices are you prepared to make for your children, if you are blessed with any? What sacrifices would you make for the children of your brothers or sisters or friends? for children you don't even know?

• Joseph, Mary, and Jesus had to leave in the middle of the night and move to Egypt. Did you and your family ever move anywhere? If so, did you like it? If not, do you know anyone who has moved into your town or city?

• If you had to move to a new place, what would you want to take with you? Would you want to leave in the middle of the night? Why or why not?

• What nice things does your family do for you? What helpful things do you do for your family?

Closing

They expected a general . . .
   And were given a child.
      They expected a coronation . . .
         And were given a star.
            They expected victory . . .
               They were given love!

(Richard Fanolio)

Feast
of the Holy Family

29 December 1996
26 December 1999
29 December 2002

Blessings
for Families

Scripture

- *Sirach 3:2–6,12–14.* Children are asked to love and bring honor to their parents.
- *Colossians 3:12–21.* Wives, husbands, children, and parents: Love one another.
- *Luke 2:22–40.* Simeon and Anna recognized the baby Jesus as the Savior.

Theme

Part of God's plan for parents and children is for them to love and serve one another. When Mary and Joseph were performing their purification ritual at the Temple, they were approached by two people. Simeon was assured by the Holy Spirit that he would not die before he saw the Christ. And Anna was a prophet who lived at the Temple, fasting and praying, day and night. They both recognized that this baby was the One they had been waiting for, and they told his parents wondrous things about him.

Focusing Object
A picture of your family

Reflections

For Adults

Families need a lot of support these days. Parenting was never a simple job, but the pressures of our modern society have made it even more stressful. For this reason it is a blessing for a parent to hear words of praise about his or her child. Moreover, it is a gift for us to go out of our way to affirm parents when we have seen their children behave well, make difficult decisions, serve others, or do other things a parent would be proud of.

- Do you know of families who have done a good job of "being family"? Do you know a young person or child who is obviously taught and guided lovingly by a parent? Have you observed a young person or child doing something a parent would be proud of? What good things might you tell the parent about this son or daughter?
- When you were a child, did you ever overhear any praise about yourself that some adult was telling your parent? If so, what was it? How did you feel? If not, what was something you did that you know your parent was proud of, or would have been proud of?
- If you are a parent, what things does your child do that make you feel proud? Do you affirm your child often enough? What is one thing you can tell a child more often that will affirm her or him?

For Teenagers

No doubt Mary and Joseph were surprised and pleased, and perhaps even a bit spooked, when these complete strangers approached them at the Temple to praise their baby.

- Has your parent ever been surprised and pleased, or even spooked, when someone else came and told them some wonderful thing about you? What was it? What do you do that your parent (stepparent, grandparent, or guardian) is proud of?

Just as parents love to hear good things *about* their sons and daughters, they also love to hear good things *from* their sons and daughters.

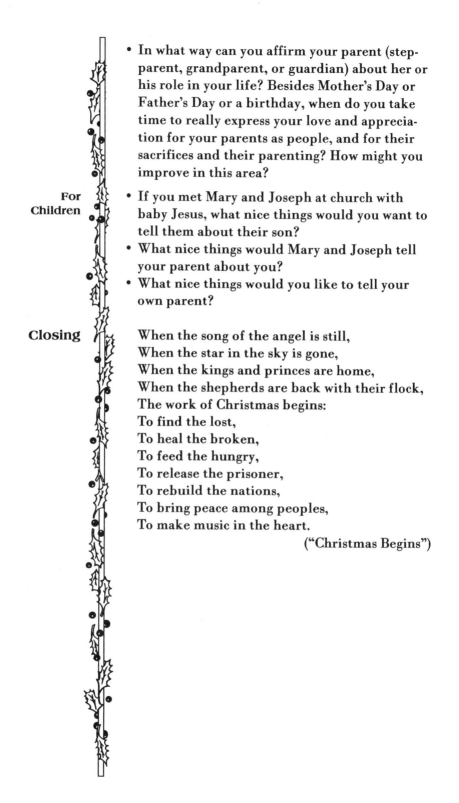

- In what way can you affirm your parent (step-parent, grandparent, or guardian) about her or his role in your life? Besides Mother's Day or Father's Day or a birthday, when do you take time to really express your love and appreciation for your parents as people, and for their sacrifices and their parenting? How might you improve in this area?

For Children

- If you met Mary and Joseph at church with baby Jesus, what nice things would you want to tell them about their son?
- What nice things would Mary and Joseph tell your parent about you?
- What nice things would you like to tell your own parent?

Closing

When the song of the angel is still,
When the star in the sky is gone,
When the kings and princes are home,
When the shepherds are back with their flock,
The work of Christmas begins:
To find the lost,
To heal the broken,
To feed the hungry,
To release the prisoner,
To rebuild the nations,
To bring peace among peoples,
To make music in the heart.

("Christmas Begins")

C

Feast of the Holy Family

28 December 1997
31 December 2000
28 December 2003

Family Life

Scripture

- *Sirach 3:2–6,12–14.* Children are asked to love and bring honor to their parents.
- *Colossians 3:12–21.* Husbands, wives, children, and parents: Love one another.
- *Luke 2:41–52.* Mary and Joseph searched for Jesus for three days in Jerusalem.

Theme

Although Nazareth had no junior high schools, Jesus was junior high age when his parents lost him. His parents were traveling with extended family, and they could not find Jesus among any of the relatives. Frantic, they walked a day's journey back to Jerusalem and searched all over the city for him. After *three days* they found him in the Temple, where he was discussing matters of faith with the teachers. His parents could not understand how he could be so calm about the matter—didn't he realize what they had been through looking for him? And he did not seem to understand why they hadn't expected to find him there at the Temple. A typical case of parent-teen miscommunication. The Holy Family was a lot like most other families! How comforting!

Focusing Object
A picture of your family

Reflections

For Adults

- Did you ever get lost as a child? Do you remember hearing stories about your parents or other relatives trying to find you? Do you remember being frightened?
- If you are a parent, was your child ever lost for any significant amount of time? Do you remember trying to figure out where she or he could have gone? Were you frightened? Were you angry? How did you finally locate your child?
- Is it hard for you to imagine Jesus doing something that his parents would disapprove of? Do you naturally assume that Jesus was the "perfect" child, forgetting he was a normal human being and had to grow up like the rest of us? Is it easy to picture the Holy Family just like your holy family?

For Teenagers

Picture yourself in Jesus' situation. You have been sightseeing with your parents at the festival in the big city, and your parents are on their way home. They have been traveling for a day and cannot find you. They turn around, walk back to the city, and search for you for three days before they find you talking to the priests in a church!

- What would your parents say to you? What would you say to them? How much trouble would you be in? Where would you have stayed for those days you hadn't seen them? What would you have been thinking?
- Is it fun to think that Jesus "got in trouble" with his parents too? Sometimes we get so hung up on Jesus as *Almighty God* that we forget about Jesus as a *human being*. What other things do you think Jesus must have done as he grew up—things we don't usually think about, things not recorded in the Bible?

For Children

When Jesus was twelve years old, he wandered off from his parents. They could not find him for three days.

- What do you think would happen if you wandered away from your parents for three days? What would they say to you when they found you? How would they feel? How would you feel?

When Jesus was your age, he probably acted a lot like you. He had to learn how to read, he had to obey his parents, he probably got cranky when he was tired, and he probably liked to eat desserts.

- If Jesus was your age and was in your class, and he was your best friend, what kind of things do you think he would do with you?

Closing

Peek A Boos
I Love Yous
Knick Knacks
Secret Pacts
Skating Parties
Pretend Dating
Boy Girl Fights
Mosquito Bites
Grimy Hands
Too Much Fun
Yesterday
("What is a childhood?" by Kelly Milbourn,
a high school student)

Solemnity of Mary, Mother of God

1 January, every year

The Wonder of It All

Scripture

- *Numbers 6:22–27.* May God bless you and keep you.
- *Galatians 4:4–7.* Jesus, born of woman, has come to redeem us.
- *Luke 2:16–21.* Mary reflected on all that had happened.

Theme

The first day of each year is a day to honor Mary, the mother of Jesus. It is a day to look ahead to a brand new year, as Mary looks ahead to a brand new life. It can also be a day to look back on the past year, on its struggles and hurts as well as its successes and celebrations. With both the looking ahead and the looking back, it is appropriate to be aware of our blessings, and to make use of our ability to bless. Native Americans of many tribes bless themselves and one another with the holy smoke from burning sage and sweet grasses. Often a feather is used to guide the smoke in the direction of the person being blessed.

Focusing Object
Incense and, if possible, a feather

Reflections

For Adults

As Mary reflected on all the happenings centered around the birth of her son, she no doubt had mixed emotions. When we look back on the year we have just completed, some events will have upset us and some will have delighted us. Some events may have occurred that we did not appreciate at the time, and we may wish we had paid more attention to them as they were happening.

* What are some upsetting events, delightful events, or unappreciated events that took place in the past year?
* As Mary reflected on the birth of her son Jesus, she no doubt dreamed about the future as well as the past. What dreams do you think she might have had for him and for their family? What dreams have you had for yourself and your family?

For Teenagers

The beginning of a new year is a time when TV shows, radio shows, and magazines look back at the year that has just passed. Mary, too, spent time reflecting upon all the happenings surrounding the birth of her son.

* What events of the past year do you think were most significant in the political world? in the sports world? in the entertainment world? in your family life? in your personal life? in your spiritual life?
* The first of the year is also a time for making yearly predictions. Lots of celebrities like making predictions for the year ahead. What do you predict for the political world? for the sports world? for the entertainment world? in your family life? in your personal life? in your spiritual life?
* Who has been a real blessing to you this past year?

For Children

* What things can you remember from the past year? Can you remember Easter? Can your remember your birthday? Can you remember last summer? What were some of the best things that happened during the year? Did anything really sad happen? If you want to, talk about what it was like.

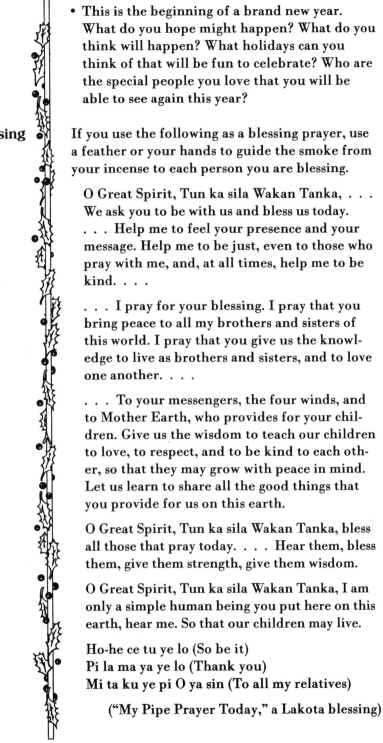

• This is the beginning of a brand new year. What do you hope might happen? What do you think will happen? What holidays can you think of that will be fun to celebrate? Who are the special people you love that you will be able to see again this year?

Closing

If you use the following as a blessing prayer, use a feather or your hands to guide the smoke from your incense to each person you are blessing.

O Great Spirit, Tun ka sila Wakan Tanka, . . . We ask you to be with us and bless us today.
. . . Help me to feel your presence and your message. Help me to be just, even to those who pray with me, and, at all times, help me to be kind. . . .

. . . I pray for your blessing. I pray that you bring peace to all my brothers and sisters of this world. I pray that you give us the knowledge to live as brothers and sisters, and to love one another. . . .

. . . To your messengers, the four winds, and to Mother Earth, who provides for your children. Give us the wisdom to teach our children to love, to respect, and to be kind to each other, so that they may grow with peace in mind. Let us learn to share all the good things that you provide for us on this earth.

O Great Spirit, Tun ka sila Wakan Tanka, bless all those that pray today. . . . Hear them, bless them, give them strength, give them wisdom.

O Great Spirit, Tun ka sila Wakan Tanka, I am only a simple human being you put here on this earth, hear me. So that our children may live.

Ho-he ce tu ye lo (So be it)
Pi la ma ya ye lo (Thank you)
Mi ta ku ye pi O ya sin (To all my relatives)

("My Pipe Prayer Today," a Lakota blessing)

Epiphany

Following
the Star

5 January 1997
4 January 1998
3 January 1999
2 January 2000
7 January 2001
6 January 2002
5 January 2003
4 January 2004
2 January 2005

Scripture

- *Isaiah 60:1–6.* Camels bringing gold and frank-incense will follow the light.
- *Ephesians 3:2–3,5–6.* The Gentiles are heirs with the Jews.
- *Matthew 2:1–12.* Astrologers followed the star, found Jesus, and brought him gifts.

Theme

Isaiah foretold that nations would gather to follow the light and offer gifts. The story of the Magi has glamour, danger, and courage. It is a story of accepting the journey to an unknown place; following the star because of faith. And it is a story of Gentiles coming to visit Jews, bringing gifts, and being welcomed.

Focusing Object
A star, or a tray with gold (jewelry), frankincense (incense), and myrrh (skin oil)

Reflections

For Adults

In the story of the Magi we are dealing with an extraordinary child. The star is so brilliant that astrologers follow it in faith—not knowing who they will find, but needing to make the journey. "Following a star" has become a metaphor for following your dream, pursuing your calling, or making an ideal you believe in become a reality.

- What star have you followed? What dream might you still be pursuing? What ideal do you believe in and work toward?

The ones who had faith and followed the star to worship the newborn Messiah were not Jews but Gentiles! It was unheard of for Jews and Gentiles to mix, but these Gentiles came, brought gifts, and were welcomed into the home.

- What do you think is the significance of Gentiles rather than Jews being featured in the Epiphany story?
- Name a group you never thought you would mix with, a group toward whom you now feel tolerant, accepting, and understanding. What is it like reflecting on your change of heart? How did it come about?
- Name a group you still have difficulty accepting. What might it take for you to have a change of heart? Is it possible?

For Teenagers

The astrologers in the Magi story went through quite a journey in search of the baby Jesus. They obviously believed in him and had faith in the star.

- Have you ever "followed a star"? Have you ever gone after a dream or an ideal you believed in? Are you still going after it? What gives you the energy to keep going? How do you know it is worth it?

The gifts brought by the Magi have significance. *Gold* is a symbol of wealth and fidelity. *Frankincense* is burned to purify the atmosphere by releasing an aromatic and pleasing smell. For centuries, Native Americans have burned holy smoke in order to bless and purify themselves, and monks have watched incense rise to the sky as a symbol of their prayers ascending to God. *Myrrh* is a kind of resin or oil used for anointing and embalming. It is a symbol of comfort and soothing (who doesn't enjoy a rubdown?) but it is also a foreshadowing of death.

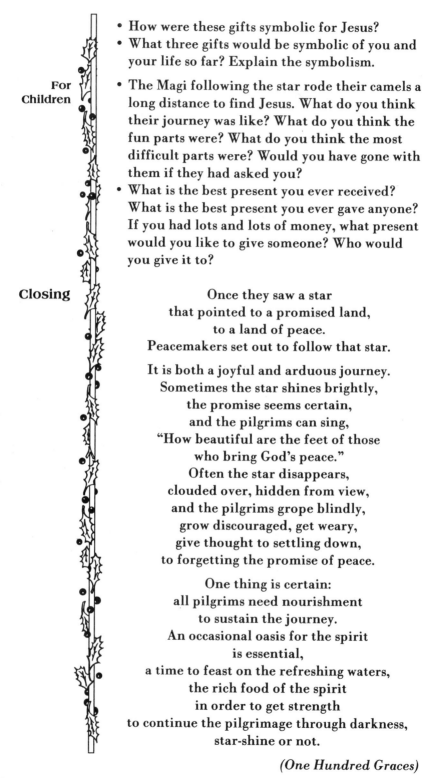

- How were these gifts symbolic for Jesus?
- What three gifts would be symbolic of you and your life so far? Explain the symbolism.

For Children

- The Magi following the star rode their camels a long distance to find Jesus. What do you think their journey was like? What do you think the fun parts were? What do you think the most difficult parts were? Would you have gone with them if they had asked you?
- What is the best present you ever received? What is the best present you ever gave anyone? If you had lots and lots of money, what present would you like to give someone? Who would you give it to?

Closing

Once they saw a star
that pointed to a promised land,
to a land of peace.
Peacemakers set out to follow that star.

It is both a joyful and arduous journey.
Sometimes the star shines brightly,
the promise seems certain,
and the pilgrims can sing,
"How beautiful are the feet of those
who bring God's peace."
Often the star disappears,
clouded over, hidden from view,
and the pilgrims grope blindly,
grow discouraged, get weary,
give thought to settling down,
to forgetting the promise of peace.

One thing is certain:
all pilgrims need nourishment
to sustain the journey.
An occasional oasis for the spirit
is essential,
a time to feast on the refreshing waters,
the rich food of the spirit
in order to get strength
to continue the pilgrimage through darkness,
star-shine or not.

(One Hundred Graces)

Baptism of the Lord

A: 10 January 1999
13 January 2002
B: 12 January 1997
9 January 2000
12 January 2003
C: 11 January 1998
not celebrated in 2001
1 January 2004

Baptized in the Spirit of God

Scripture

Note: The first two readings are the same for all three cycles for the feast of the Baptism of the Lord. The Gospel reading changes for each cycle.

- *Isaiah 42:1–4,6–7.* Behold the Chosen One, on whom I have poured my Spirit.
- *Acts 10:34–38.* The word was proclaimed, beginning with the baptism John preached.
- *Matthew 3:13–17* (A); *Mark 1:7–11* (B); *Luke 3:15–16,21–22* (C). At Jesus' request, John baptized him, and the voice of God expressed pleasure.

Theme

John the Baptizer is preaching a baptism for repentance. But John announces that Jesus will baptize with the Holy Spirit. In John's time people came forward, were brought into the river to be immersed with the water, and then they were helped out. It was more than a shower—it was an underwater journey. Each person entered the death of not being able to breathe. Each person emerged into the new breath and cleanliness of refreshing, full life.

Focusing Object
Water in a pitcher

Reflections

The church is making an effort to return to the full symbolism of water in baptisms. Years ago, infants were just sprinkled with a drizzle of water; adults just held their head over the font to receive the drizzle. Unless you were standing close, you could not tell any water was present. But today, more and more, churches are putting in baptismal pools so children and even adults are able to stand in the font and have a pitcher of water poured over them.

• Have you seen such a baptism? What was your impression of the fullness of the water symbol? Did it have more impact than just a drizzle? Share your feelings.

• Have you ever been asked to be a godparent? If so, what was it like to see the baptism and know that you had a special relationship to that person's faith development?

Baptism was so important that even Jesus came forward to be baptized. And the voice of God was heard to give approval. Obviously, Jesus had no need for repentance.

• Why do you think he wanted to begin his public ministry with his own baptism?

Try to imagine what it would be like on a hot and dry day to go to the river and be baptized by John the Baptizer. Try to imagine being drenched with water as you make a new commitment to life without sin. Then imagine seeing Jesus, the one John has been preaching about. He gets baptized himself, and the skies open up and a dove alights on him, and you hear the voice of God announce pleasure with what Jesus has done.

• What would you do next? How is your life different when you take that experience seriously? How is your life different now because of your baptism?

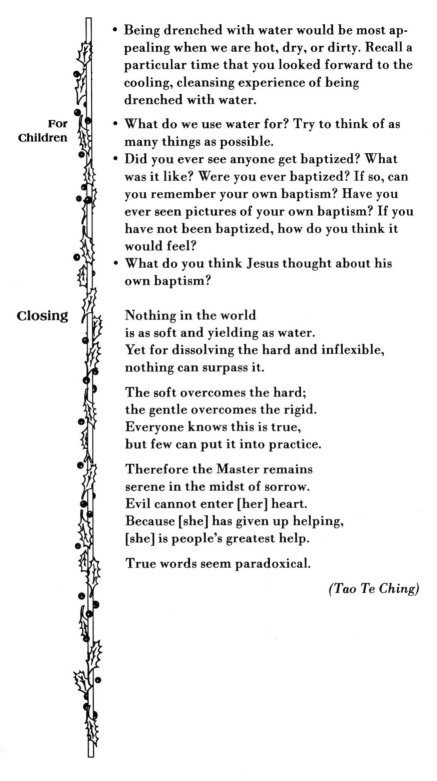

- Being drenched with water would be most appealing when we are hot, dry, or dirty. Recall a particular time that you looked forward to the cooling, cleansing experience of being drenched with water.

For Children

- What do we use water for? Try to think of as many things as possible.
- Did you ever see anyone get baptized? What was it like? Were you ever baptized? If so, can you remember your own baptism? Have you ever seen pictures of your own baptism? If you have not been baptized, how do you think it would feel?
- What do you think Jesus thought about his own baptism?

Closing

Nothing in the world
is as soft and yielding as water.
Yet for dissolving the hard and inflexible,
nothing can surpass it.

The soft overcomes the hard;
the gentle overcomes the rigid.
Everyone knows this is true,
but few can put it into practice.

Therefore the Master remains
serene in the midst of sorrow.
Evil cannot enter [her] heart.
Because [she] has given up helping,
[she] is people's greatest help.

True words seem paradoxical.

(Tao Te Ching)

Lent

First Sunday of Lent

25 February 1996
21 February 1999
17 February 2002

The Serpent

Scripture

○ *Genesis 2:7–9; 3:1–7.* The serpent tricked Adam and Eve, and they disobeyed God.
• *Romans 5:12–19.* Adam and Eve brought sinfulness; Jesus brings righteousness.
• *Matthew 4:1–11.* The devil tried to tempt Jesus, but he was not tricked.

Theme

The serpent is an old symbol of evil. It can strike suddenly and quickly, or it can enter slowly over a period of time. It can strike suddenly and catch us off guard, or slither into our lives and slowly choke the goodness out of us. We humans often give in to sin, but Jesus showed us how to live a life of righteousness.

Focusing Object
A rubber or wooden snake, or a picture of a snake

Reflections

For Adults

• Does evil sneak into your life slowly, so that you do not even notice you have developed a sinful habit? Or does a tempting situation catch you off guard, so that you are suddenly involved in something you should not be?
• If evil is so sneaky, how do you defend against it in your life? How do you recognize it and what do you do about it? Are the strategies for

resisting slow, sneaky evil different from the strategies for resisting quick, striking evil?

For
Teenagers

Peer pressure works like a snake. Sometimes it is a slow process, and without realizing it you just gradually start doing things and saying things and thinking things that your friends do, say, and think. Sometimes it is a quick strike and you are suddenly in a situation and have to make a choice. Some friends are trying to get you to do one thing and some are trying to get you to do something else. Peer pressure can be negative or positive.

- Which kind of negative peer pressure are you more likely to be influenced by—the slow, gradual type or the high-pressure, fast type?
- Which kind of positive peer pressure are you more likely to be influenced by?
- Can you give an example of when positive or negative peer pressure influenced you?
- Do you ever use positive peer pressure to influence others? Do you think you are more likely to influence others slowly, over the long haul, or quickly, in a sudden or specific situation? Can you give an example of when you have had a positive influence on another person?

For
Children

- Some snakes are harmless and they cannot hurt you. Other snakes are very dangerous. Because it is hard to tell the dangerous snakes from the harmless snakes, what is a good thing to do if you see a snake?
- Here are some good ways to learn about snakes: go to a zoo, read a book about snakes, or watch a TV show about snakes. What do you already know about snakes? What do they eat? How do they eat? When are they dangerous to people?
- In the Bible story, a snake talks to Adam and Eve. Do you think this really happened or do you think it is the kind of story that helps us learn something? What do you think this story about a snake and two people is trying to teach us?

Closing

From the time they can herd a goat,
From three years and nine months on,
Maybe earlier,
    The smallest African child can spot a snake
        lying on a rock,
        way up in a tree,
        just slithering into an ant hill.
Never,
Never,
Never a quick move, around a corner,
        under a low branch,
        through tall grass.
Have you ever felt your hair
    stand up
    seeing snake signs on soft ground,
    digging into a pile of stones,
    moving through an abandoned hut?
You feel python-chatu around springs,
        puff adders in corn fields,
        green mamba on low branches.
The kids in Old Blue
    yelled:
Don't run over it.
Don't injure it.
It'll attack someone, if injured.
We saw a full-sized,
        head-up,
        slow-moving,
        clear-across-the-road
Black mamba
    and stopped to ponder,
        to remember,
        to be Adams and Eves.
In the Serengeti
    We joke about lions,
    We warn about cape buffalo,
    We laugh at hyena,
but we have one eye alert
    for broods of viper,
        sunning serpents,
        SNAKES.

Like our baby chicks sense
   hawks day one,
     immediately,
     by the shadow,
So Africans
   All-Adam-and-Evekind sense
     The serpent instinctively,
     biblically,
     by adder antennae.

(Don Larmore)

First Sunday of Lent

16 February 1997
12 March 2000
9 March 2003

The Rainbow in the Clouds

Scripture

○ *Genesis 9:8–15.* God tells Noah that the rainbow is a sign of the Covenant.
• *1 Peter 3:18–22.* The waters of the ark and the waters of baptism
• *Mark 1:12–15.* John the Baptizer is arrested; Jesus preaches the Good News.

Theme

In Noah's day, only a few were saved from the waters. Today, all can be saved with the waters—the waters of baptism. Lent is a time to repent and believe in the Good News—the Good News that began when God told Noah about the Covenant. The Covenant is marked by the rainbow.

Focusing Object
Any object with a rainbow on it

Reflections

For Adults

God makes the same covenant with you that is made with eve ry living creature and with all future generations. The covenant includes people of all races, from every nationality, from every walk of life, and with all kinds of personalities.
• Is there a certain person or a certain group of people that gives you a hard time? Is it difficult for you to see him, her, or them with you

as the rainbow children of God? Why do you think that is?

- God speaks of the "covenant between me and the earth." That implies a relationship of harmony with all forms of life in our environment. In what ways are you aware of your connection with, and your responsibility for, the environment? What steps can you take to improve your relationship with the forms of life and the planet we have in common?
- The Scriptures tell us that God made a covenant with you and every living creature that is with you, for all future generations. How is your life different when you take God's covenant seriously?

For Teenagers

A rainbow is a symbol of diversity in harmony. In a rainbow, the individual colors are unique, but they blend together and form a beautiful unity. Being a "Rainbow People" means we are a people of diversity who live together in harmony.

- Can you think of people who are different from you yet live in the harmony of friendship with you? How are they different from you? How are these differences a blessing to your friendship?
- A rainbow is a symbol of covenant, a symbol of promise, a symbol of faithfulness. Have you ever broken a promise? Has anyone ever broken a promise to you? Have you ever had an experience of unfaithfulness in a friendship? What happened?
- God said the rainbow was a sign of the covenant between God and the earth. How is your relationship to our planet earth and all of its life? What are some of the problems human beings are creating for other forms of life, and what are some things you can do to help solve those problems?

For Children

- Have you ever seen a real rainbow in the sky? Where did you see it? What were you doing at the time? What was it like?
- God said the rainbow was a sign of the covenant between God and all of us. A covenant is a promise of love. Who are some people you love? What do they do for you that shows how they love you?
- In a rainbow, all the colors are different, but they are all beautiful. Even though people are all different, each person is beautiful to God. Look at the people around you now. How is each person different from you? How is each person beautiful in a different way?

Closing

We are the rainbow people.
We are the rainbow people.
We are beams of golden light.
We are the bridge to the dawning of a new day.
   ("Rainbow People," a Native American chant)

First Sunday of Lent

1 March 1998
4 March 2001
29 February 2004

The Desert

Scripture

- *Deuteronomy 26:4–10.* Yahweh took us from slavery in Egypt, through the desert, to a new land.
- *Romans 10:8–13.* We who believe in Jesus and speak of Jesus will be saved.
- *Luke 4:1–13.* Jesus spends forty days and nights alone in the desert.

Theme

Jesus knows what it is like to be in the desert and to want God's help. He had his own desert experience, being tempted by the devil, feeling alone and isolated, and needing strength and faith. It happened to the Hebrews, it happened to Jesus, and it happens to us. Desert experiences can be retreats for us if we use them as a way to get closer to God.

Focusing Object
Sand

Reflections

For Adults

The path to a closer relationship with Yahweh, our Creator, is the faith journey of every human being. The Holy Spirit is every human being's instigator of that journey and its guide. Even though Jesus is fully divine, Jesus is also fully human. So why does Jesus have to go on such a desert journey to get closer to God? Jesus *is* God. Wouldn't that mean he was going on a journey to get to himself? Isn't that what all of us do when we need to get closer to God, too?

- Where do you go to seek Yahweh, our creator? How do you become closer to the One who made you? How do you get closer to yourself? What happens on the journey to yourself? How do you know you are traveling in the right direction?

- When were you in a "desert experience"? When have you found yourself feeling alone, isolated, and in need of strength? When have you struggled in your journey back to Yahweh? When have you had a "waiting room time" for you to sit it out in the desert and be patient, and hope for the rich fertile awareness of God's presence to return?

The Hebrews were not happy with their slavery in Egypt. But they were not thrilled with being isolated in the desert land, either. In some ways, that was worse. But Jesus actually chose to retreat into the desert land. He followed the guidance of the Holy Spirit in his life and ended up in the desert for a long time.

- Have you ever felt as if you were in a desert, alone and isolated—escaped from an old place perhaps, but not yet arrived at a new place? Which was worse—the place you had escaped from or the desert place? Why? What moved you to get on with your life journey in order to actually arrive at the new place? Or are you still in the desert? How do you know?

- Jesus retreated to the desert because the Holy Spirit led him there. Has the Spirit ever led you to a place that ended up being a desert? Did you ever do "the right thing" and end up alone and isolated? What happened? Were you surprised? angry? at peace? How does the bareness of desert-life give way to the rich fullness of growth-life?

- Is there anything good about a desert experience? Without other distractions, all you have is yourself and God. In that situation, is it easier or harder to get closer to God?
- Is it possible to become more in touch with God and not become more in touch with yourself? Why or why not? How does being in touch with yourself help your relationship with God? How do you get in touch with yourself?

For Children

- Jesus stayed alone in the desert for forty days. The Bible tells us that he did not eat any food all that time. How hungry do you think he became? How would you feel if you tried to stay in a desert that long without eating? What would you say to Jesus if you found him in the desert?
- Do you ever play at a beach or in a sandbox? Do you like to play in sand? What is it like? What do you do in the sand? How does dry sand change when it gets wet? What can you do with wet sand that you cannot do with dry sand? What does dry sand do that wet sand does not do? Is it more fun if you can use water with the sand? Why or why not? Is it messier? What is the best part about playing in sand?
- Potting soil is special soil that makes plants grow better. If you planted some flowers in a sandbox and other flowers in rich, dark, potting soil, which flowers do you think would grow? Why do you think so? Have you ever planted flowers in sand? in potting soil? What do you think the potting soil does that the sand cannot do?
- Not many plants can grow in the desert sand, but some can. Do you know what kinds of plants grow in a desert? Do you know what kinds of animals might live in a desert?

Closing

How strong and good
　　and sure your earth smells,
　　and everything that grows there.

Bless us, our land,
　　and our people.

Bless our forests with mahogany,
　　wawa and cacao.

Bless our fields
　　with cassava and peanuts.

Be with us in our countries,
　　and in all of Africa,
And in the whole world.

(*Peace on Earth*, a prayer from the Ashanti
people of Africa)

Second Sunday of Lent

3 March 1996
28 February 1999
24 February 2002

Abraham (Abram) and Sarah's (Sarai's) Journey

Scripture

- ○ *Genesis 12:1–4*. God tells Abram and Sarai to journey to a new land.
- • *2 Timothy 1:8–10*. God calls us to a holy calling.
- • *Matthew 17:1–9*. Transfiguration: Jesus took Peter, James, and John up a mountain.

Theme

God calls us to journey. Sometimes we arrive at a beautiful mountaintop, seeing miraculous visions. Other times, we never seem to arrive. We seem to journey on and on with no destination, no order, no plan. We journey because we trust God, and God calls us to a holy calling.

Focusing Object
A suitcase, knapsack, or travel bag

Reflections

For Adults

Abram and Sarai had to completely trust God, who told them that their names would be blessed and that they would begin a great nation. They did not know any details of any plan, and they were uncertain of any destination.

- • Have you ever been on a journey like that? Where has God led you? When was it most difficult to trust God?
- • Do you know where God is leading you now? What keeps you on the journey? How can you tell when God is "calling you to a holy calling"?

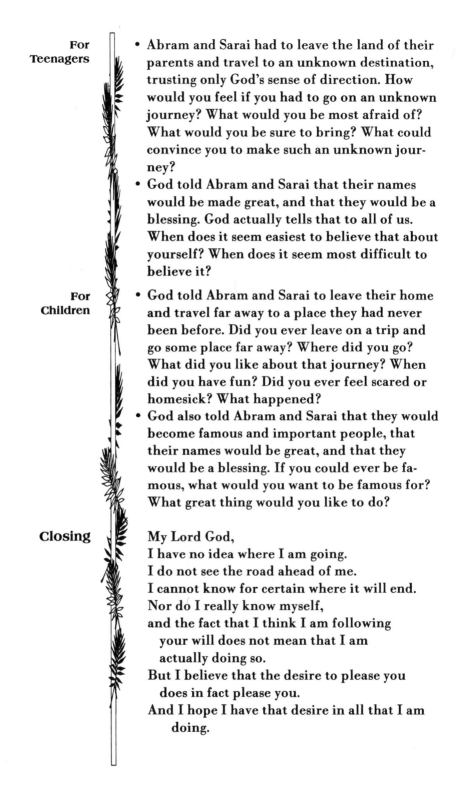

For Teenagers

- Abram and Sarai had to leave the land of their parents and travel to an unknown destination, trusting only God's sense of direction. How would you feel if you had to go on an unknown journey? What would you be most afraid of? What would you be sure to bring? What could convince you to make such an unknown journey?

- God told Abram and Sarai that their names would be made great, and that they would be a blessing. God actually tells that to all of us. When does it seem easiest to believe that about yourself? When does it seem most difficult to believe it?

For Children

- God told Abram and Sarai to leave their home and travel far away to a place they had never been before. Did you ever leave on a trip and go some place far away? Where did you go? What did you like about that journey? When did you have fun? Did you ever feel scared or homesick? What happened?

- God also told Abram and Sarai that they would become famous and important people, that their names would be great, and that they would be a blessing. If you could ever be famous, what would you want to be famous for? What great thing would you like to do?

Closing

My Lord God,
I have no idea where I am going.
I do not see the road ahead of me.
I cannot know for certain where it will end.
Nor do I really know myself,
and the fact that I think I am following
    your will does not mean that I am
    actually doing so.
But I believe that the desire to please you
    does in fact please you.
And I hope I have that desire in all that I am
    doing.

I hope that I will never do anything apart
   from that desire.
And I know that if I do this,
you will lead me by the right road though I
   may know nothing about it.
Therefore will I trust you always though I
   may seem to be lost and in the shadow
   of death.
I will not fear, for you are ever with me,
and you will never leave me to face my perils
      alone.

("The Road Ahead")

B

Second Sunday of Lent

23 February 1997
19 March 2000
16 March 2003

The Transfiguration

Scripture

- *Genesis 22:1–2,9,10–13,15–18.* Abraham sacrifices a ram instead of his son Isaac.
- *Romans 8:31–34.* If God is with us, who can oppose us?
- *Mark 9:2–10.* Peter, James, and John see Jesus transfigured on the mountain.

Theme

Abraham's experience of God was so strong that he was willing to do anything God wanted. Peter's insight into the mystery of Jesus in the Transfiguration was so strong that he wanted to stay on the mountaintop and revel in it. Yet, God led them beyond these experiences. If God is with us, who can oppose us?

Focusing Object
A crystal sun catcher, or a bright white napkin or cloth with an aluminum foil "star" or "sun" stapled or sewn to it

Reflections

For Adults

Peter, James, and John had a "mountaintop" experience, something they did not want to leave behind. It was beyond their wildest imagination.
- Have you ever had a "mountaintop" experience? a place or situation or view that was so dazzling that you wish you could just build

yourself a dwelling and stay there with the glory and wonder of it all?

• God said Jesus was a Beloved Son and we should listen to him. How is your life different when you take God's words seriously?

• Have you ever experienced a place or situation that was breathtaking, incredible, glorious, and awesome? something you did not want to leave behind? something that filled you with joy and life and zeal? What was it like? Where was it? What made it so special? Were you alone or with others? Were you able to explain it to someone who was not there? Why or why not?

• Why do you think Jesus wanted Peter, James, and John to experience him as a glistening, dazzling, transfigured vision? How do you think that affected their faith? How would it have affected your faith? How does if affect your faith just reading about it?

• Peter did not want to leave that mountaintop experience. He wanted to build some booths and just "camp out" there for a while. Why was it better for Jesus and Peter and the others to come down from the mountain? Why is it important for us to enjoy and remember our "peak" experiences, but leave them behind and come back to our everyday life?

• What is the most dazzling, glistening, sparkling, bright thing you have ever seen? What was it like when you saw it?

• If you were with Jesus and he became dazzling and glistening, how do you think you would feel? Would you be excited and full of "zeal"? What would you say? Would you be like Peter and want him to stay that way? Or would you want him to change back to the normal Jesus? Why?

Closing

Implant within my heart, O Jesus
  the fiery zeal of Peter,
  the conviction of Moses and Elijah,
  and the love of James and John.

Stir my slumbering soul,
  that it might sing a song of passion and
    devotion,
  excited with dancing joy and desire for you,
  my divine and loving and dazzling Friend.

May I be consumed with zeal for you,
  for life, for justice and for peace;
  for all that I know in faith.

Fill me with zeal, O Jesus.

(Adapted from *Prayers for a Planetary
Pilgrim*, a prayer for zeal)

Second Sunday of Lent

8 March 1998
11 March 2001
7 March 2004

Stars

Scripture

○ *Genesis 15:5–12,17–18.* Abram will have descendants as numerous as the stars.
• *Philippians 3:17—4:1.* This dazzling Jesus is in heaven; our earthly bodies will be changed to match his glorious body.
• *Luke 9:28–36.* Jesus is transfigured before Peter, James, and John.

Theme

Abraham and Sarah, both old and childless, look at the stars and see children and grandchildren too many to count. Peter, James, and John look at Jesus and see him beside Moses and Elijah in a sight too brilliant to stare at for long. If God is on our side, how can we fear whomever or whatever is against us?

Focusing Object
Any picture or object with stars or constellations on it

Reflections

For Adults

• Ever since time began, people have looked to the stars for inspiration, for guidance, and for perspective. What inspires you? What guides you? What gives you perspective? Share a story about a time you were inspired or guided or received needed perspective from the stars or from another source.

- Abraham and Sarah were old and childless, and they longed for children. If you are a parent, think of your own children. If not, think of nieces or nephews or neighborhood children. Are they like the stars to you? Can they inspire you, give you perspective, or guide you? What effect do children have on the very old or even the moderately old?
- Abraham and Sarah believed in the impossible dream that Yahweh promised them. Is there an impossible dream that you believe in? What is it? Why does it seem impossible? Why do you still believe in it?

For Teenagers

Abraham and Sarah were old and childless, and they longed for children. Descendants, like stars, meant to them a permanent place in history, because their names would be carried on. Today, a "star" is a celebrity, someone with a name that is well known. In fact, people often confuse "stars" with "heroes." Just because a person is famous and well known does not mean that person is a good role model for people.

- Who are your heroes? Are they "stars"? What makes them heroic in your opinion?
- When you stare up at the stars at night, what do you think of? life on other planets? alien creatures and UFOs? TV shows and movies based on space travel? astronomy? astrology? How do the stars affect your imagination?

For Children

Abraham and Sarah were very old and they did not have any children. They really wanted children, so when God promised them children, they believed God.

- Why do you think Abraham and Sarah wanted children? Why do you think anyone desires to have children? What would the world be like without children? Who do you know that really loves children a lot? What is he or she like?
- Have you ever looked up into the night sky to see the stars? What do they look like? What do you like best about stars? How many do you think there are?

Closing

We are the stars which sing
We sing with our light.
We are the birds of fire
We fly across the heaven,
Our light is a star.
We make a road for Spirits,
A road for the Great Spirit.

(*Peace on Earth*, a prayer from the Algonkian
people of North America)

Third Sunday of Lent

The Woman at the Well

Scripture

- *Exodus 17:3–7.* In the desert, Moses strikes the rock, and water flows for his people.
- *Romans 5:1–2,5–8.* Through Jesus and our faith we can have peace with God.
- *John 4:5–42.* Jesus meets the woman at the well who leads many to believe in him.

Theme

The need for water led Moses to beg God on behalf of his people. God sent water flowing from a rock. The need for water led the Samaritan woman to the well, and to an encounter with Jesus. Jesus sparked her curiosity when he told her of the living water he could provide. Jesus' story must have worked! The woman left her bucket behind in her zeal to tell others about him. Though she was a sinner, her faith in Jesus brought her forgiveness and peace.

Focusing Object
An empty water bucket

Reflections

For Adults

That famous woman at the well does not even have a name, but she sure upsets any notion that only holy people do God's work. Though sinful and unholy, she is unmatched in her excitement for spreading the good news about the Messiah

99

and gaining followers for him. She captures our imagination. Who could have known what a powerhouse she was, and how evangelizing she could be?

- Is there anyone in your life that you used to think of as "unholy" or "uncultured," but now see the worth of that person? Is there anyone you used to think of as a weed, yet now see as a flower? Why did your opinion and your relationship change?
- Jesus says that whoever drinks of the water that he shall give, will never thirst; the water he gives will become in that person a spring of water welling up to eternal life. How might life be different when this message is taken seriously?

For Teenagers

The woman at the well did not ask Jesus for a favor. Jesus asked her for a favor. She had the bucket. He wanted a drink. She has had five husbands and is living with a sixth man. She is a Samaritan and a woman—both characteristics a Jewish man was raised to look down on. Yet, she dares to question and argue with Jesus. As rugged as she is, she recognizes what is special in Jesus and she wants that living water he is talking about. She is so convinced he is the Messiah that she leaves her bucket behind as she runs off to tell others the good news. She won Jesus so many followers that he stayed with them for two days. She is a weed, a flower, and a rebel, all rolled into one.

- Do you know anyone like the Samaritan woman—someone who seems so unholy and so holy at the same time? someone hard to figure out? Do you feel like that sometimes? Why or why not?
- Jesus came to turn weeds into flowers, and wallflowers into movers and shakers. Share about a time you were most flower-like, a time you were most weed-like, or a time you were most rebel-like.

Some people did not like the woman at the well,
but Jesus talked with her, and he liked her. Jesus
likes everyone, even people who do not have a lot
of friends.
- When you meet someone new, how do you feel?
  Do you feel shy and not want to talk much? Do
  you feel outgoing and want to be friendly?
  When was a time you met someone new?

In certain places where there is a lot of grass
you often find dandelions. Dandelions are hard
to figure out. Lots of children like dandelions
because they are pretty and bright yellow. But
lots of grown-ups do not like dandelions because
they are weeds and their seeds spread easily.
- Have you ever played in the grass and found
  dandelions? Have you ever felt like a dande-
  lion in the grass?
- Sometimes we feel like flowers, and sometimes
  we feel like weeds. When do you feel more like
  a flower? When do you feel more like a weed?

Closing

Her head bowed low
Fertile with seed
The stately flower
Basks in the warm sun
Long and lean
Lionistic mane
A blue ribbon winner
She graces the plains
No sweet scent does she give
No tender care does she need
For she's branded a rebel
A flower and a weed
    ("Ode to the Sunflower," by Kelly Milbourn,
                           a high school student)

Third Sunday of Lent

B

26 March 2000
23 March 2003

The Ten Commandments

Scripture

○ *Exodus 20:1–17.* God delivers the Command-ments to Moses.
• *1 Corinthians 1:22–25.* God's folly is wiser than our wisdom.
• *John 2:13–25.* Jesus drives the money changers out of the Temple.

Theme

Even people who hate rules and regulations can-not deny that the Ten Commandments are a pretty good foundation for moral behavior. We still need God's wisdom to guide our folly and our sinful ways. No doubt folly and sinful ways were on Jesus' mind as he watched the money changing and marketing going on at the Temple.

Focusing Object
A rule book, law book, student handbook, orga-nization bylaws, or list of class or family rules
(If your class or family does not have a list of rules, this might be an opportunity to ask the members to come up with a list of the rules that are routinely followed and expected of them. Making that list together could be your actual faith sharing. Or, if it is made ahead of time, the list can be used as a focusing object.)

Reflections

- Which of the Ten Commandments is the most important? Which is hardest (or used to be hardest) for you to keep? Which is easiest for you to keep?
- How do you feel about rules and laws in general? Do you appreciate them for the order they keep? Or do you find them a burden for the freedom they restrict?
- It is often said that today's "false gods" are expensive cars, clothes, guns, vacations, and other status indicators. God tells us not to make gods out of things. How is your life different when you take this message seriously?

No matter what the rule or law is, some people can find a way around it. Sometimes they obey the "letter" of the law, but they disregard the "spirit" of the law. Sometimes they pretend to misunderstand the meaning of the law. And sometimes they actually get away with breaking a law by paying off someone who is supposed to be guarding the law.

- Is it ever okay to break a law? Why or why not? Give some examples.
- What are some school rules or family rules that you hate to keep? What do you dislike about them? What are some school rules or family rules that you wish other people would keep, but they don't? Why do you like those rules?
- Do you think it would be possible to run a country, a school, an organization, or a family without rules or laws? Why or why not? How would life be different?

- What are some rules you do not like? Why don't you like them?
- What are some rules you do like? Why do you like them?
- What would happen if nobody followed any rules?

- If you could make some rules of your own, what rules would you make?
- Why do you think God gives us rules to follow?

Closing

We take time to thank You
  for those common tasks that we must
    perform each day,
  those necessary labors of life
  by which, according to Your Divine Plan,
  we are also to create the Kingdom here in our
    midst.

. . . .

Help us, Lord our God,
  to use the work of this day—
  to perform it with mindfulness and
    attention,
  with care and devotion—
  that it will be holy and healing
  for us and for all the earth.

("Blessed Are You, Lord, Our God,
Who Enhances Our Lives with Work")

Third Sunday of Lent

C

15 March 1998
18 March 2001
14 March 2004

The Burning Bush

Scripture

- ○ *Exodus 3:1–8,13–15.* God spoke to Moses in the flames of a burning bush.
- • *1 Corinthians 10:1–6,10–12.* The events of Moses have meaning in our lives, too.
- • *Luke 13:1–9.* The gardener gives the barren fig tree another year to bear fruit.

Theme

Yahweh speaks to Moses in a bush that is on fire but is not burning up. Moses, an exile from Egypt for having killed someone there, is called back to lead the people he deserted. The fig tree, which has not given any figs, is given another year to bear fruit. Moses' second chance is like the fig tree's second chance and like our second chance. And Yahweh, who created us, calls to us from within a flame and urges us to begin again.

Focusing Object
A lighted candle

Reflections

For Adults

Moses is fascinated with the fire that burns but does not consume the bush. The God of the burning fire calls him. He goes. We are fascinated with a God whom we love and fear.

- Why do people fear God? Why do people love God? Do you love or fear God? Why? Have you ever been fascinated with a call from God? Have you ever been afraid of a call from God? What happened?

Yahweh tells Moses he is standing on holy ground. Holy ground is the place where we meet the Divine, the Holy; where we meet God; where we meet ourselves. Yahweh is calling Moses to go back to free the people who gave him birth; to return to the land where he is known to have killed a person. Having met God, Moses cannot hide from God or himself.

- When do you want to hide from the One who created you? When have you been on holy ground? When have you met Yahweh, face-to-face, and known who you are?
- Have you ever felt that Yahweh was giving you a "second chance"?

For
Teenagers

- The bush is on fire, but it is not burning anything. Moses is fascinated with that. Have you ever watched a campfire, a fireplace, or a candle with fascination? Do you know anyone who has? What is so fascinating about flames? What is so fascinating about our God?
- Moses is getting a second chance at greatness. He would actually rather stay where he is, with the flocks at Midian, but Yahweh has greater plans for him. Have you ever gotten a second chance? Did you feel relieved? Did you feel burdened? What happened? Did you need a third chance?

For
Children

- Why is fire dangerous? Have you ever gotten burned? What happened?
- Moses noticed a bush that was burning, but was not getting burned up. When Moses went over to look at the burning bush, do you think he was careful? Why? What do you think he did? What would you have done?

• Fire can be helpful. When Moses was alive, there was no electricity and there were no heaters or microwave ovens. How do you think fire helped people then? Can you think of ways that God helps people in the way fire does?

Closing

Fire is your sacrament, O God, fire is sacred;
  As I light this candle may I be reminded
   that I am to burn with the same fire for you.
May I fill my life with that burning love.

(Prayers for a Planetary Pilgrim,
a candle prayer)

Fourth Sunday of Lent

The Man Born Blind

Scripture

- *1 Samuel 16:1,6–7,10–13.* God sees differently; young David is anointed king.
- *Ephesians 5:8–14.* Before you were in the dark; now you are in the light.
- *John 9:1–41.* Jesus heals a man born blind; the Pharisees remain blind.

Theme

God chooses Jesse's youngest son David to be anointed as the new king, even though others do not "see" David's potential yet. When Jesus heals a man born blind, it is clear that he who was blind was able to "see" more clearly than the Pharisees, who supposedly have excellent sight. We all have been given the light of faith to see with; no longer spiritually blind, no longer walking in spiritual darkness.

Focusing Object
A pair of glasses

Reflections

For Adults

It is almost annoying to read in this story how the Pharisees treated the man who was born blind. They were so bent on finding fault with Jesus, they could not see the miraculous gift Jesus was. They focused on all the wrong things.

- Have you ever been so intent on seeing one thing that you failed to see another? Has your spiritual blindness ever caused a problem for you? What happened?
- Have you ever had a problem with your eyes or your vision? For example, did you ever lose a contact lens? break your glasses? have surgery on your eyes? get an eyelash in your eye? How did you cope with your situation?
- If you are physically blind, talk about what it is like. Which do you think is worse: a person's physical blindness or other people's "blind attitudes" toward a person who is physically blind? What can be done about such attitudes? How can we respond when such attitudes are obvious and blatant?

For Teenagers

- Stevie Wonder, the famous singer and musician who is blind, once remarked that just because a man lacks the use of his eyes doesn't mean he lacks vision. What do you think he meant? What do you think we need to learn from him?
- Jesus cured a man born blind. That man had more "vision" than the Pharisees, who could see. What do you think Jesus was trying to teach us about spiritual and physical blindness?
- What is the most incredible thing you have ever seen: a lunar eclipse? a rainbow? a shooting star? a peacock showing off its feathers? a butterfly on a flower? fireworks? How could you describe this incredible sight to a person who is blind?
- What do you think would be the most difficult part of being blind? If you are blind, talk about what the most difficult part is for you.

For Children

Jesus healed a man who was born blind. That man was sure that Jesus was from God. He was sure because only God could do such a wonderful thing. But the Pharisees would not believe him. They would not believe Jesus either. The Pharisees were afraid that if people believed that Jesus was from God, then all the people would follow Jesus rather than themselves.

- If you were there, what would you say to the Pharisees? What would you say to the man who had been born blind? What would you say to Jesus?
- Do you know anyone who is blind? Do you know what the Braille alphabet is? Have you ever seen anyone read Braille, use a Braille typewriter, or walk with a Seeing Eye dog? If you did, tell what it was like.

Closing

Creator God, Holy Parent,
  We rejoice in our eyes,
  These two tiny but marvelous gifts
  That add so much to the fullness of our lives.
This gift of sight enlarges the world of our
      enjoyment
  And magnifies our appreciation of nature,
  Of great works of art,
  Of the gifts of books and printing,
  Of those persons we love,
  And for this we are grateful.
We thank You also for the gift of insight
  By which our spirit sees and understands.
We are especially thankful for Your Son, Jesus,
  Who opened the eyes of the blind
  And gave to a weary world New Sight.
Blessed are You, Creator God,
  For this wondrous gift of sight.
(Adapted from "Blessed Are You, Lord Our God,
                for the Wondrous Gift of Sight")

Fourth Sunday of Lent

9 March 1997
2 April 2000
30 March 2003

God's
Handiwork

Scripture

- *2 Chronicles 36:14–17,19–23.* God has compassion for us and sends prophets.
- ○ *Ephesians 2:4–10.* We are God's handiwork.
- *John 3:14–21.* God so loved the world, that Jesus came to us.

Theme

We are God's handiwork. The immeasurable riches of God's own grace and kindness are given to us. We are precious to God, who sends us prophets to guide us and Jesus to save us. Our work reflects the handiwork of the One who made us, the One who prepared the path for us to walk.

Focusing Object
Any handmade craft object

Reflections

For Adults

- If God prepared a path for us beforehand, that we might walk on that path, how do we know if we are walking on the right path? What are the signs in your life that tell you when you are and when you are not walking on the right path?
- The Scriptures say that we are God's handiwork, created in Christ Jesus for good works. Do you feel like God's handiwork? Is your life filled with good works? How is your life different when you take this message seriously?

- Being God's handiwork means God took great pride and care in creating us. What are some of your gifts and talents—characteristics that God takes great pride in? Do you feel awkward when you are asked to list your gifts and talents? Why or why not?

- We were created in Christ to do good works. What are some good works you have already participated in? What are some needs in your school, in your family, in your neighborhood, in your country, and in your world? What is one good work you can focus on doing in the near future?

- God created a path for us beforehand, so that we might walk on it. Do you think God created a very specific path for each individual? Or do you think God created a very general path of goodness so that each individual might find his or her own way to walk? Explain your answer.

- Have you ever made anything out of clay or out of paper? Have you ever cooked or baked something? Have you ever sewn something? What was it like? How did you feel after it was finished?

- God made us so we could do good things for others. What are some good things you did today? What are some good things you might do tomorrow?

Closing

God of all handiwork,
> We love to create things, and we love the things we create.
> The bits of ribbon, the lumps of clay, the specks of glitter.
> We like to dab paint, and sew buttons, and sprinkle with spices.
> Our creations help us feel proud and accomplished.

But you have created life!
You have made every living, breathing, growing creature!
You have made each of us. We are your handiwork.
Our bones, and hair, and blood, and skin! Our brains and our hearts!
Help us to do the good works you created us for. Amen.

Fourth Sunday of Lent

22 March 1998
25 March 2001
21 March 2004

The Prodigal Child

Scripture

- *Joshua 5:9,10–12.* Yahweh told Joshua that the reproach of Egypt was rolled away.
- *2 Corinthians 5:17–21.* We need to be reconciled to God.
- ° *Luke 15:1–3,11–32.* The prodigal one returned to a feast; the other one was jealous.

Theme

The guilt from the days in Egypt is forgiven. Our God is a forgiving God. Jesus tells us the story about a family member who sinned and was greeted with presents and a party upon returning home. The prodigal wasn't even sorry—just merely hungry and tired and looking for a way to get basic needs met! But forgiveness is bountiful with Yahweh. We need that reconciliation. And it is waiting for us.

Focusing Object
A gift-wrapped present

Reflections

For Adults

- If you have children, picture yourself as the parent in the story of the prodigal. Would you have been as forgiving of the child who returned, penniless and dirty? Would you have been as generous? What would you have said to the child who did not appreciate the return of the prodigal?

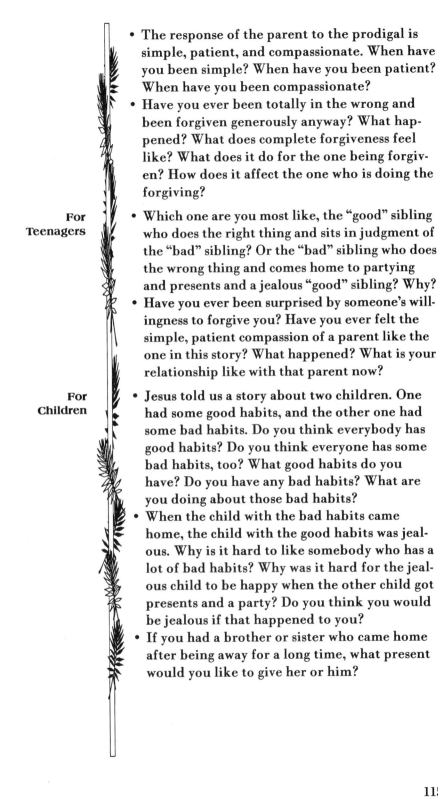

- The response of the parent to the prodigal is simple, patient, and compassionate. When have you been simple? When have you been patient? When have you been compassionate?
- Have you ever been totally in the wrong and been forgiven generously anyway? What happened? What does complete forgiveness feel like? What does it do for the one being forgiven? How does it affect the one who is doing the forgiving?

For Teenagers

- Which one are you most like, the "good" sibling who does the right thing and sits in judgment of the "bad" sibling? Or the "bad" sibling who does the wrong thing and comes home to partying and presents and a jealous "good" sibling? Why?
- Have you ever been surprised by someone's willingness to forgive you? Have you ever felt the simple, patient compassion of a parent like the one in this story? What happened? What is your relationship like with that parent now?

For Children

- Jesus told us a story about two children. One had some good habits, and the other one had some bad habits. Do you think everybody has good habits? Do you think everyone has some bad habits, too? What good habits do you have? Do you have any bad habits? What are you doing about those bad habits?
- When the child with the bad habits came home, the child with the good habits was jealous. Why is it hard to like somebody who has a lot of bad habits? Why was it hard for the jealous child to be happy when the other child got presents and a party? Do you think you would be jealous if that happened to you?
- If you had a brother or sister who came home after being away for a long time, what present would you like to give her or him?

Closing

I have just three things to teach:
simplicity, patience, compassion.
These three are your greatest treasures.
Simple in actions and in thoughts,
you return to the source of being.
Patient with both friends and enemies,
you accord with the way things are.
Compassionate toward yourself,
you reconcile all beings in the world.

(Tao Te Ching)

Fifth Sunday of Lent

24 March 1996
21 March 1999
17 March 2002

Lazarus Raised from the Dead

Scripture

- *Ezekiel 37:12–14.* God will open our tomb and raise us from the dead.
- *Romans 8:8–11.* God who raised Jesus will raise us also.
- *John 11:1–45.* Martha believes Jesus is the Messiah; Jesus raises Lazarus from the dead.

Theme

Death is a natural part of life. It can be frightening and painful to think about death. We may be afraid to die. We may fear being left alone when a loved one dies. But there is still good news—we will be raised up. Ezekiel told us that was how we would know God. Jesus raised up Lazarus; Jesus himself was raised up.

Focusing Object
A picture of a relative who has died

Reflections

For Adults

Martha declares that Jesus is the Messiah, the son of the Living God. Mary tells Jesus she believes that had he been there sooner, Lazarus would never have died. Still, they were probably not expecting Jesus to raise their brother from the dead. But Jesus told them that if they believed, they would see the glory of God.

- How is your life different when you take your faith seriously?

117

Jesus' raising of Lazarus was a bit different than Jesus' own Resurrection. Even though Lazarus was raised from the dead, we can safely assume that he eventually died again. However, not so with Jesus. His was not merely a resuscitation. His everlasting life was in a different sort of body, and so will ours be. Even though our faith gives us comfort in the face of death, there is still anxiety.

- When it comes to dealing with death, what is the hardest struggle for you?
- Do you have a relative that has died? If so, how did this relative enrich your life? What characteristics of her or his do you share?

For Teenagers

- Do you have a relative that has died? If so, how did this relative enrich your life? What characteristics of hers or his do you share?
- Our faith comforts us in the face of death, because we believe that we will be raised up, like Jesus. What do you think about that? How does it feel to think about your own death or the death of someone you care about?

For Children

(If you are in a group with people who do not know the deceased relative whose picture you are using, then tell them his or her story and how you came to choose this relative for today's prayer sharing.)

Martha and Mary were Lazarus's sisters. They were good friends with Jesus, and they knew he was God. They missed their brother and were very sad when he died. They did not know Jesus was going to bring Lazarus back to life!

- What do you think Martha and Mary said to Lazarus when he came out of the grave? What do you think Lazarus said to Martha and Mary later on when he had the chance to talk with them?

We believe that we will be in heaven with Jesus after we die. But even so, dying is very sad. When a person dies, everyone is sad because they miss that person.

Closing

• Can you remember someone who has died?
What do you remember about that person?

We are born asleep and at death we awake.
(the Prophet Mohammed
from the Koran)

Your visionary son, Mohammed,
reminds me this day, O God,
that I am a sleepwalker
who wanders through life
with eyes closed to the glory of your presence.
Lift my drooping eyelids this day
from the slumber of the unawakened,
so that I might see you
in the vastness of the universe.
Oh, that I might be awakened this day
to see how your glory fills all of heaven and
earth.
I pray that I need not wait until death
to behold your divine face,
to feel your embrace,
and to live in your blessed presence.

(Adapted from *Prayers for a Planetary Pilgrim,*
a prayer from the Islamic tradition)

Fifth Sunday of Lent

16 March 1997
9 April 2000
6 April 2003

The Grain of Wheat

Scripture

- *Jeremiah 31:31–34.* You will be our God, we shall be your people.
- *Hebrews 5:7–9.* Jesus is the source of eternal salvation.
- *John 12:20–33.* Only the seed that dies can produce fruit.

Theme

Being people of God means being people who have faith in life after death. Jesus taught us this with his story of the grain of wheat that dies and then produces new life in its fruit. He also shows us life after death by rising from the dead.

Focusing Object
Wheat seeds, or any type of seed

Reflections

For Adults

- Our faith is very much based on life after death. The stories of our lives are filled with examples of wheat seeds that die, and the resulting fruit that blooms. Where in your life have you experienced life after death?
- The Scriptures tell us that those who love their lives above all else will ultimately lose them, but those who lose their lives in this world will keep them for eternal life. How is your life different when you take this message seriously?

Part of growing older is learning how to accept
the experiences of loss in our lives, and to have
hope in the experiences of growth and new life
to come. Experiences of loss could be felt when
moving to a new town, after the breakup of a
close relationship, or after the death of a friend
or relative. Experiences of growth and new life
could include meeting new friends in a new
town, having a different but honest relationship
with someone you care about, or feeling peaceful-
ness in your heart with the memory of someone
who has died.

- What are some experiences of loss in your life
  that have been followed by experiences of
  growth or new life?

Jesus said the ones who serve would follow him
and the ones who would lose their lives would
live forever.

- What do you think these words of Jesus are all
  about?
- What does it mean to follow Jesus?
- What do you think it means to lose life in order
  to live forever?

**For
Children**

- If you put a seed in the ground, and you water
  it, does it stay just a seed, or does it turn into
  something else? What does a tomato seed turn
  into? How about a pumpkin seed? What about
  a cucumber seed? Could an apple seed ever
  grow and become a watermelon? Why not?
- Have you ever been to a vegetable garden?
  What was it like? What are your favorite vegetables?
- Did you ever plant a seed? What kind of seed?
  What happened? Would a new plant grow if
  the seed just stayed a seed? Why not?

121

Closing

The seed of God is in us.
Given an intelligent and
hardworking farmer, it will
thrive and grow up into God,
whose seed it is; and accordingly
its fruits will be God-nature.
Pear seeds grow into pear trees,
nut seeds into nut trees, and
God seeds into God.

(One Hundred Graces)

Fifth Sunday of Lent

29 March 1998
1 April 2001
28 March 2004

Jesus Saves a Woman Who Sinned

Scripture

- *Isaiah 43:16–21.* It is time to consider something new; old ways are over.
- *Philippians 3:8–14.* We can forget what lies behind us and focus on what lies ahead of us.
- *John 8:1–11.* Jesus saves a woman from being stoned to death.

Theme

The old law said that some sins were so bad, the sinner ought to be stoned to death. Jesus had a new law to teach us—a law of compassion and forgiveness. We all are sinners, and we need to help one another rather than destroy one another. We can hate the sin, but we need to love the sinner. It is never too late for us to learn a new way. This new way saved a woman's life.

Focusing Object
A stone

Reflections

For Adults

That old law was a tough one. It said if you find someone in an adulterous relationship, you are to throw stones at them until they are dead. Jesus helped a group of judgmental, angry men see that all of us are sinners. Often those who judge others most harshly are most guilty of the sin they see in others.

Have you ever wondered where the man in that adulterous relationship was? If they caught the woman in the act, why were they only trying to stone the woman? Had the men in that crowd committed the same sin, but without being caught?

- What characteristics or habits are you most judgmental of? What part of those flaws can you claim? What relationship makes you the most angry? How do you contribute to the problems in that relationship? What can you do that you are not doing? What are you doing that you should not be doing?
- How do you contribute to the violence of the world? How do you contribute to the peace of the world?

- Have you ever been caught doing something you knew was wrong? What happened?
- Have you ever done something with a friend of yours, and your friend got away with it, but you didn't? How did you feel? Did you want your friend to get into trouble as well? Or were you thankful that at least both of you didn't get caught?
- What sins, mistakes, or faults from the past would you like to forget? What stops you from letting go of them and moving on? What new ways or new habits would you like to be yours from now on?
- Jesus stopped a mob of men from stoning a woman to death. They could easily have turned on him, but they did not. Why do mobs want to commit acts of violence? Why do you think violence has become such a major part of the entertainment business, such as movies, video games, and so forth? What is fun about violence?

For Children

Jesus saw a group of men who were angry with a woman. They wanted to throw stones at her and hurt her. Jesus stopped them because it is wrong to hurt anyone, no matter how angry we are.

- What do you do when you are angry? Do you remember a time that you were angry at something or somebody? What happened?
- It is not right to throw stones at anyone. It is never okay to hurt anyone in any way. But it can be fun to throw stones into a lake or a field, or a place where the stones won't hit a person or animal or damage property. Have you ever thrown stones? Where? Did you like it? Why or why not?
- Some people collect rocks and stones. There are different kinds. Have you ever seen a rock collection? Whose was it? What did your favorite stones look like?

Closing

Violence is something we have seen in our daily, family life. Come, Lord and make each of us see that force is rarely the right answer to problems. Teach us to talk to each other, to listen carefully, to touch lovingly and to care greatly for all and each one in our family.

("Teach Us in Love," a Lakota prayer)

Passion Sunday (Palm Sunday)

31 March 1996
28 March 1999
24 March 2002

The Rooster Crowed

Scripture

- *Isaiah 50:4–7.* Although suffering, I shall not be put to shame.
- *Philippians 2:6–11.* Every knee should bend at the name of Jesus.
- ○ *Matthew 26:14—27:66.* Peter denied Jesus three times before the cock crowed.

Theme

Jesus told Peter that he would deny knowing Jesus three times before the rooster crowed. Peter tried to blend into the crowd, but he was recognized as a Galilean. Even if the people did not see what he was up to, it seemed that he could not hide. He would be found out. The rooster crowed. Peter was guilty and he knew it.

Focusing Object
A plastic or ceramic rooster or a picture of a rooster

Reflections

For Adults

Richard McBrien, a theologian, likes to speak of an old Latin maxim, *Res clamat domino,* meaning "a thing clamors for its owner." The maxim describes the notion of an internal alarm system in the world. McBrien then coined his own maxim, *Iustitia clamat donec satisfacta,* meaning "Justice clamors until it is satisfied" *(National Catholic Reporter).*

Peter is devastated when he hears the rooster. He hears justice clamoring, and he is guilty.
- Have guilt feelings ever called you to right a wrong? Have peaceful feelings ever filled you after you righted a wrong?

Biblical language connects nature to justice in other places, for example, the blood of Abel cries out in Genesis 4:10, and all creation groans in Romans 8:22. Beyond the rooster, nature participated in the story of Jesus' Passion in other ways—for instance, the animal Jesus rode, the palms cut down, the crown of thorns, the tree Jesus was nailed to. Nature as well as justice was at unrest. When we sin, nature is often dragged in as an unwilling accomplice. And much of our sin is sin against nature—disrespect for God's creation shown by abuse of persons, pollution, waste of natural resources, and the like.
- How are we different when we see our actions as being connected to nature—to God's creation?

For Teenagers

Peter is devastated when he hears the crowing of the rooster. It is as if the rooster watched him, heard his denials of Jesus, and cried out for justice to be done.

Imagine the earth witnessing and suffering with every act of injustice: the night stars seeing Judas betray Jesus, the grasses being crushed as Jesus falls to the ground carrying the cross, all the trees feeling the awful pounding of the nails of crucifixion, and the earthquake trembling when Jesus dies.
- Is this point of view far-fetched, or does it contain some truth? Can you imagine the organic planet at unrest with all the violence done to people and to nature? Or do you view most of nature as unfeeling, inanimate matter, more or less disconnected from us?

127

- So often we think it is "okay" to do something if we "don't get caught." If you see that your decisions affect all of nature, how would it change the attitude of "try to get away with whatever you can"?

For Children

When the rooster crowed, Peter remembered what he had done wrong. The Bible says he was so upset, he went out and cried.

- Have you ever been so upset over something you did that you ran someplace and cried? How did you start to feel better? What do you think Peter did?
- Some people think that animals can tell when things are not right. When Jesus was being hurt and crucified, do you think there were animals around? What kind of animals? Do you think they could sense that something was wrong?

Closing

Note: Mention that in the following prayer it is the earth that is talking to God.

My God,
why?
Have you
forsaken me?
Have you
forgotten
the work
of your
hands?
Poured out
like sand—
dry,
lifeless,
without
hope,
I call
out to
you:
save me!

Remember, God,
that at your command,
I provided from my elements
the flesh and blood of the savior.
I fed, sheltered and clothed his body.
And for the salvation of the world I, too,
though innocent, was crucified with him.
I mourned, anointed, and entombed him.
I, I alone, witnessed his most holy rising.
Yet I am treated with utter contempt—
torn, abused, scourged and violated.
How long, O Lord, must I and all
creation await deliverance?
Turn our death throes
into birth pangs.

Behold the wood of the cross and know that I,
the Earth, participated in the life, death and
resurrection of the Lord. And I, reliquary and
womb, will one day, with the heavens, be re-
newed.

("Prayer of Earth Crucified")

Passion Sunday (Palm Sunday)

23 March 1997
16 April 2000
13 April 2003

The Crucifixion

Scripture

- *Isaiah 50:4–7.* God helps us endure the pain we cannot escape.
- *Philippians 2:6–11.* Jesus humbled himself to accept death on the cross.
- *Mark 14:1—15:47.* Jesus is betrayed, crucified, and dies.

Theme

To follow Jesus means to accept pain we can hardly bear. It means to humble ourselves to powerlessness. It means to keep on loving even when we are betrayed and abandoned. And it means to continue the celebration of life, even when death threatens.

Focusing Object
A cross or crucifix

Reflections

For Adults

- Try to recall when you first learned about the Crucifixion of Jesus—long ago, when you were a child. What were your thoughts and feelings?
- Even Jesus called out to God in anguish and complained that he was being forsaken and forgotten. In the midst of great suffering, have you ever felt as if God had forgotten you? What were the circumstances of that suffering? Was there eventually any growth or new life?

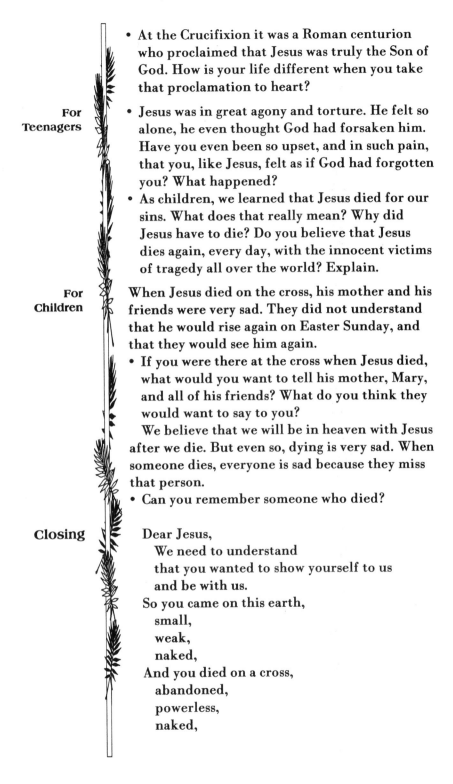

- At the Crucifixion it was a Roman centurion who proclaimed that Jesus was truly the Son of God. How is your life different when you take that proclamation to heart?

For Teenagers

- Jesus was in great agony and torture. He felt so alone, he even thought God had forsaken him. Have you even been so upset, and in such pain, that you, like Jesus, felt as if God had forgotten you? What happened?
- As children, we learned that Jesus died for our sins. What does that really mean? Why did Jesus have to die? Do you believe that Jesus dies again, every day, with the innocent victims of tragedy all over the world? Explain.

For Children

When Jesus died on the cross, his mother and his friends were very sad. They did not understand that he would rise again on Easter Sunday, and that they would see him again.

- If you were there at the cross when Jesus died, what would you want to tell his mother, Mary, and all of his friends? What do you think they would want to say to you?

We believe that we will be in heaven with Jesus after we die. But even so, dying is very sad. When someone dies, everyone is sad because they miss that person.

- Can you remember someone who died?

Closing

Dear Jesus,
  We need to understand
  that you wanted to show yourself to us
  and be with us.
So you came on this earth,
  small,
  weak,
  naked,
And you died on a cross,
  abandoned,
  powerless,
  naked,

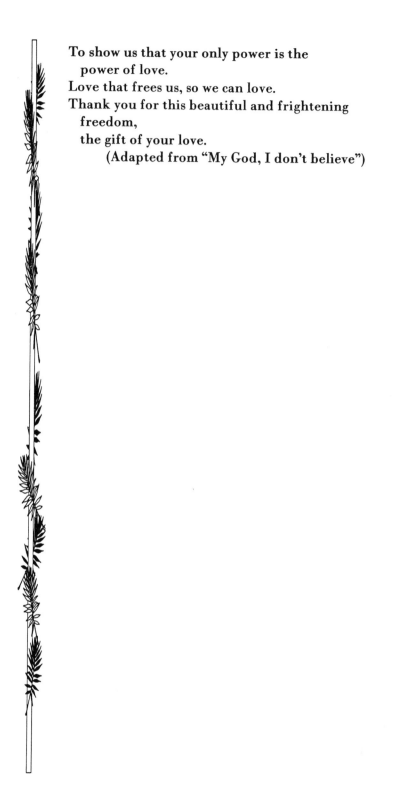

To show us that your only power is the
  power of love.
Love that frees us, so we can love.
Thank you for this beautiful and frightening
  freedom,
    the gift of your love.
        (Adapted from "My God, I don't believe")

Passion Sunday (Palm Sunday)

Divine Forgiveness

Scripture

- *Isaiah 50:4–7.* Suffering can increase compassion; violence is dealt with peacefully.
- *Philippians 2:6–11.* Jesus, our savior, humbled himself, even to innocent death on a cross.
- *Luke 22:14—23:56.* Jesus forgives those who show violence to him.

Theme

Jesus is mocked, beaten, tortured, and finally killed. He forgave every violent act committed against him. He healed the slave's ear cut by his disciple; he forgave the soldiers who drove the spikes into his body, and he forgave the thief hanging beside him. No sin is too great for his divine forgiveness.

Focusing Object
Three nails

Reflections

For Adults

It is hard to imagine such forgiveness. Jesus forgave those who were killing him, even as it was happening. Jesus' response to violence was peace and forgiveness, not even self-defense.

- What kind of faith and strength does it take to follow such a radical leader? What are your feelings about nonviolent resistance to conflict? How do you see yourself responding to violence from another person?

- Who was the person you had the hardest time forgiving? What situation made you, or makes you, so angry, it cannot be forgotten? Was there, or is there, a wrong and a hurt in your life so deep that you still have a hard time letting go and forgiving? How can that affect your relationship with yourself, with others, and with God?

For Teenagers

It is hard to imagine the kind of violence that took Jesus' life. It is hard to imagine having spikes pounded into your wrists, and hanging from a crossbeam so you can hardly breathe. It is hard to imagine having people watch you struggle in pain and mock you as you die. It is hard to imagine anyone purposefully inflicting death on another person. It is even harder to imagine a victim of that pain forgiving everyone who took part in it.

- What would be hardest for you—enduring the physical pain? forgiving the enemies causing you the pain? forgiving the friends who deserted you?
- Who in your life has been the person hardest to forgive? What has been the most hurtful thing ever done to you? What has been the most difficult situation for you to recover from? What can you learn from Jesus' example that can help you when it is hard to forgive?

For Children

It took a lot of different people to kill Jesus. It took some people in charge, like Pilate and Herod, and it took soldiers and crowds of angry people. A lot of people wanted to kill Jesus even though he had never hurt anyone. Maybe they were afraid of Jesus. Maybe they were jealous of him. Maybe they were so mixed up inside, they did not know what they were doing. But Jesus forgave them all, even the ones who never said they were sorry.

- What would you want to say to Herod and Pilate and the soldiers? What would you want to tell them about Jesus? What would they say if they talked to you?

- Has anyone ever hurt you or hurt your feelings? What happened? Did they ever say they were sorry? Did you forgive them? Are you friends now, or are you still mad at them? What was it like?

Closing

Knowing others is intelligence;
knowing yourself is true wisdom.
Mastering others is strength;
mastering yourself is true power.

If you realize that you have enough,
you are truly rich.
If you stay in the center
and embrace death with your whole heart,
you will endure forever.

(Tao Te Ching)

Easter Time

Easter Sunday

7 April 1996
30 March 1997
12 April 1998
4 April 1999
23 April 2000
15 April 2001
31 March 2002
20 April 2003
11 April 2004

The Folded Linen Cloths

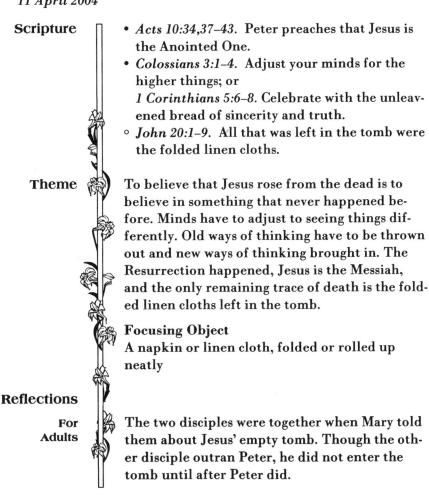

Scripture

- *Acts 10:34,37–43.* Peter preaches that Jesus is the Anointed One.
- *Colossians 3:1–4.* Adjust your minds for the higher things; or
  1 Corinthians 5:6–8. Celebrate with the unleavened bread of sincerity and truth.
- *John 20:1–9.* All that was left in the tomb were the folded linen cloths.

Theme

To believe that Jesus rose from the dead is to believe in something that never happened before. Minds have to adjust to seeing things differently. Old ways of thinking have to be thrown out and new ways of thinking brought in. The Resurrection happened, Jesus is the Messiah, and the only remaining trace of death is the folded linen cloths left in the tomb.

Focusing Object
A napkin or linen cloth, folded or rolled up neatly

Reflections

For Adults

The two disciples were together when Mary told them about Jesus' empty tomb. Though the other disciple outran Peter, he did not enter the tomb until after Peter did.

- Why do you think the other disciple let Peter enter the tomb first? What makes you hesitate when you are after something? When do you allow someone else to go ahead of you?

The folded linen cloths told Mary and the two disciples that Jesus was no longer there. As yet they did not understand the Scriptures. They did not yet understand that Jesus must rise from the dead and that they, too, would rise from the dead. We have the benefit of hindsight in this matter.

- How is your life different when you take Jesus' Resurrection, and yours, seriously?

For Teenagers

Jesus' tomb was empty. It had even been cleaned up. The napkin and linen cloths were folded and rolled up neatly. Everything was left in order and taken care of. Jesus was clearly finished with this grave. No more of this "death business" for him. He left it totally behind, and was fully alive, never to know the sufferings of death again.

- Have you ever made a transition in life? Did you ever take a step and know that a part of your former life was totally behind you? What happened? How did you feel? Did you find yourself trying to take care of things or leave things in order in any way?

Obviously Mary, Peter, and the other disciple were close friends with one another and with Jesus. It is easy to picture the three of them running to the tomb together to be sure of what actually happened.

- Who are the Marys and Peters in your life? Have you ever hurried to get to some important place? Have you ever struggled with someone else to figure out what was really happening in an important situation that affected you or a friend of yours? What happened and how did that affect your relationship?

For Children

As soon as Mary told Peter and his friend that Jesus' body was not there anymore, they ran to the tomb to see for themselves. Peter's friend got there first but did not go in until Peter went in.

- If you were Mary and Peter's friend, and you ran to the tomb first, do you think you would want to go inside by yourself, or would you want to wait for your friends to catch up? Why? How would you feel? Would you be excited or scared, happy or brave?

- Do you ever help with the laundry by folding clothes? Have you ever folded your clothes or put them away while cleaning your room? How does it look when you are finished? Why do you think Jesus wanted the empty tomb to look finished, with all the cloths neatly folded?

Closing

Blessed are You, Lord our God,
   who raised Jesus up from the tomb.
We continue our celebration
   of the ever-newness of the Resurrection.
We rejoice in the Resurrection of spring,
   as birds, flowers, and fields come alive
   after the long sleep of winter.
May we share with them the Great Joy of
    Life,
   and may God's Blessing rest upon us.
(Adapted from "Table Liturgy for the Feast of
                       Easter Sunday")

Second Sunday of Easter

Doubting Thomas

Scripture

- *Acts 2:42–47.* The community of believers took care of one another's needs.
- *1 Peter 1:3–9.* Without ever having seen Jesus, we still love him.
- *John 20:19–31.* Thomas had not seen Jesus after Jesus died and had trouble believing in him.

Theme

"Seeing is believing." That could have been Thomas's motto. Jesus replies that blessed are the ones who have not seen and who still believe. We have not seen Jesus with our own eyes but our faith has led us to see him in our hearts and in one another. That kind of faith led the early Christian community to care for one another with so much zeal.

Focusing Object
A flashlight

Reflections

For Adults

"I've seen the light—I believe!" "Suddenly the light went on—I finally got it!" Light has long symbolized insight and understanding. A cartoon with a lightbulb over someone's head indicates a new idea. "A light went on" for Thomas when he actually saw Jesus, touched Jesus, and "got it."

Thomas means twin. If we see ourself as Thomas's twin, we can get even more deeply involved in his experience.

- Do you see yourself as Thomas's identical twin, as one who cannot believe what you cannot see? Or do you see yourself as Thomas's symmetrical twin, or opposite twin, one who does not have to see in order to believe? Explain why.
- Have you been "in the dark" recently about any issue or opinion? Have you recently "seen the light"? How did you change? What convinced you? Who helped "shine the light" on the situation?

For Teenagers

Thomas did not quite "get it" when the other Apostles were telling him that Jesus had risen from the dead. He wanted to see for himself. Is that really so strange? Would you believe it if your friends told you that while they were locked up in a room someone who had recently died walked through the door and appeared to them? Would you want to see it yourself?

- When it comes to Christianity, do you think you "get it"? Do you "see the light"? If so, what is it all about? If not, what don't you get? What questions do you have about Jesus' Resurrection?

The continuum of doubt and belief has two extremes. On the "extreme doubt" side is cynicism. A cynic doubts everything, especially people's good intentions. It can be a negative, unhappy way of seeing things. A person on the opposite side, the "extreme belief" side, is gullible. That person believes whatever anyone says. It can be a happy, but sometimes dangerous, way of seeing things.

- Are you a doubting Thomas? Do you think you are cynical? Do you think you are gullible? Why or why not?

- Have you ever been scared of the dark? When? How do you feel when the light goes on? Have you ever used a flashlight in the dark? Tell about what happened.
- Some things are really hard to believe. Would you believe it if someone told you they had a dog that could fly? how about a tree that had pink and blue striped leaves? What is something else you would not believe?
- Thomas had a hard time believing that Jesus was alive again. If you were one of Thomas's friends, and you had seen Jesus, what would you tell Thomas to make him believe you?

Closing

Namasté is a greeting used in Nepal and India. It is an honorable way of acknowledging another person and expressing respect, understanding, or general care. It is pronounced "Nah-Mah-STAY."

I honor the place in you in which the entire universe dwells.
I honor the place in you
which is of love, of truth, of light, and of peace.
When you are in that place in you,
and I am in that place in me,
We are one.
(Adapted from *One Hundred Graces*)

B

Second Sunday of Easter

6 April 1997
30 April 2000
27 April 2003

A Child of God

Scripture

- *Acts 4:32–35.* The community of believers cared for one anothers' needs.
○ *1 John 5:1–6.* If you believe in Jesus, you are a child of God.
- *John 20:19–31.* Thomas doubts that Jesus is alive until he sees him.

Theme

Children are trusting and easily believe what is told to them. However, like Thomas, most adults have had the experience it takes to develop more skeptical minds. Believing in Jesus and his simple message of love takes the trust of a child. Living the message of Jesus as true community and children of God is not burdensome.

Focusing Object
Any child's toy

Reflections

For Adults

- Have you ever felt old? Do you ever feel like you have lost your youth? When do you most feel that way? What causes that feeling? What do you do when that feeling comes over you? How do you respond when you hear that you are a child of God?

- We are all children of God, and we are all lovable. When do you feel most lovable? When do you feel most unlovable? Is it easier to love others as children of God than it is to love yourself as a child of God? Why or why not?

For Teenagers

- When was the last time you played with a group of small children, such as cousins, neighborhood children, or someone you were babysitting for? Did you enjoy it? What was it like? Is it easy to think of them as true children of God? Why or why not? Is it easy to think of yourself and your friends as true children of God? Why or why not?
- "God's commandments are not burdensome." Do you agree with this statement? Why or why not? Give examples of when God's commandments seem burdensome or when they do not seem burdensome.

For Children

- Do you like it when someone says you are a child of God? How does that make you feel? proud? happy? mixed up? special?
- Everyone who loves God is a child of God. Do you know any people who love God? How can you tell they love God?

Closing

Dear God,
You have given me many gifts
Trees and flowers; Rain and sunshine; Birds
   and animals.
You have given me a family and friends to love.
Please keep all these gifts safe from harm. Help
   people to love each other.
I am your child and I love you very much.
Amen.

("Children's Prayer")

Second Sunday of Easter

Write What You See

Scripture

- *Acts 5:12–16.* Many wonderful healings were done by the Apostles.
- *Revelation 1:9–19.* John is called to the gift of writing.
- *John 20:19–31.* Jesus' wonders were written down so that we might believe in him.

Theme

Jesus performed miracles, such as appearing to Thomas and the others after Jesus' death. The Apostles in the early church also performed miracles. John is called to be aware of the miracles of his time—to see the visions and recognize the hand of God, and to write down what he sees. Written words help strengthen the faith of the believers.

Focusing Object
A pen with a notebook, a diary, or paper

Reflections

For Adults

- Did you ever keep a journal or a diary? How old were you? Do you ever keep a journal now? Why or why not? What is the value of preserving the written word—how does it help us sort out thoughts or gain understanding?

147

- Do you ever have time to read books that are not directly job-related? Which books do you most enjoy? What do you think is the main purpose of those books? Is it entertainment, moral teaching, historical perspective, consciousness raising?

The Bible is a collection of books written by people who have been inspired by God to pass on our faith. It is like a family scrapbook of letters, stories, poetry, songs, and events that have influenced those we love—those who have shaped our beliefs, our lifestyles, and our prayers.

- Does your family have a scrapbook or photo album to help keep their memories? Do you think all such family collections are sacred? Why or why not?

For Teenagers

- Have you ever written in a journal or diary? Was it a hobby or an assignment from school? Was it something you kept in secret or something you shared? Did you like it? Why or why not?
- If you could write a book, what kind of book would you write—a romance novel, a science fiction book, a historical document, a how-to manual? What would be your hope for people who read your book?

The Bible is like our faith family scrapbook. It has letters, stories, poetry, songs, and information about events that have happened to the people of God ever since they became the people of God.

- Do you think the gift of writing is a calling from God? Do you think the Bible is a sacred book? Do you think all family scrapbooks and photo albums are sacred books? Why or why not?

For Children

- Do you like books? Which books are your favorites? Tell why you like those books.
- God says it is very good when people write things down. What kind of things would you like to write about? Who might like to read the things you would write about?

148

Closing

The Egyptians believed that Thoth, one of their gods, had invented writing, and they called it hieroglyphics, "the words of the god." To write a word was to be engaged in a sacred act, a ritual.

Christians call Jesus "the Word made flesh," a title which expresses the power of words to make the invisible come alive before us.

(Prayers for a Planetary Pilgrim)

We call upon Jesus, the Word made flesh, to bless our written words:
We call upon the Word to bless us:
  as we write poetry
  as we write school assignments
  as we write in our journals and diaries
  as we write proposals and reports for our jobs
  as we write letters to our loved ones
  as we write lists to help us remember
  as we write our names on legal documents and name tags and labels.

We call upon Jesus, the Word made flesh, to bless those who help provide us with the written word:
  our teachers
  our librarians
  our authors
  our publishers
  our pen pals
  our mail carriers
  our parents and family
  our friends.
Amen.

Third Sunday of Easter

21 April 1996
18 April 1999
14 April 2002

On the Road to Emmaus

Scripture

- *Acts 2:14,22–28.* Peter, filled with the Spirit, preaches that Jesus was raised up.
- *1 Peter 1:17–21.* Jesus was like the sacrificial lamb who died for us.
- *Luke 24:13–35.* Jesus meets two disciples on the road to Emmaus.

Theme

Two disciples were walking on the road to Emmaus when Jesus joined them. They told him all about their leader who had been crucified, but they did not recognize Jesus until later that evening when he was breaking bread. Then Jesus vanished. His disciples were beginning to understand that he was the sacrificial lamb who had been raised up.

Focusing Object
A loaf of bread

Reflections

For Adults

- The disciples recognized Jesus in the breaking of the bread. The way Jesus broke and blessed bread so characterized him, that it identified him to his disciples. He did it at the Last Supper, and we do it every Sunday at Mass.
- Do you think Christians can be recognized in the way they "break bread" together? How do

you break bread with your friends and family? Do you say a blessing when you are sharing a meal at home, when you are sharing a meal at someone else's home, or when you are sharing a meal at a restaurant? What conditions or situations determine how you break bread?

Jesus encountered the two disciples walking. He listened to them tell their story, and helped them understand. They broke bread together. Then he vanished, sending them back to the community to share the good news.

The four special movements are as follows:
1. Coming together
2. Listening to the story and understanding
3. Breaking bread
4. Being sent forth

These are the movements of our eucharistic liturgy, the Mass. They are also the movements of most situations with significant people in our lives. We meet, share stories, break bread, and part again.

• Can you identify these movements in your life? Have they been important in your life? What connections can you make between these movements in your relationships and these movements at liturgy?

For Teenagers

The two disciples did not recognize Jesus. But as they walked and talked with him, and listened to him explain the events of the Crucifixion in light of the Scriptures, their hearts began to burn within them.

• Has your heart ever burned within you as you recalled something you said or did? What happened?
• This story has four parts: they meet; they share stories and listen; they break bread; and they part, knowing they will see one another again. Does this sound like what you often do with your friends? How is it similar?
• Do these four movements sound like the Mass? Where is the similarity?

151

Saying "breaking bread" is another way of saying "having a meal." The saying was common in Jesus' time and culture. Most every substantial meal included loaves of bread that needed to be broken into pieces to be eaten.

- Do you like eating bread? Did you ever bake bread? Do you ever break bread into pieces, or is all the bread you eat already sliced?
- Even though the two disciples had known Jesus before, they did not recognize him when they first saw him along the road to Emmaus. Have you ever been with someone you did not expect to see again and did not recognize them because they had changed somewhat? Has your mom or dad or teacher ever had to help you recognize someone you knew at an earlier time? How did you feel? Have you ever met someone and started to talk only to find out the person did not know who you were? Did you ever have to say, "It's me! Don't you recognize me?" What was that like? Why didn't this person recognize you?

Closing

When our day comes to a close,
    and we pause to break bread together
    as the disciples on the road to Emmaus,
May our eyes be opened.

In this common act of sharing,
May we see the Risen Lord in one another.

May we see the Lord of Life in our food,
    our conversation,
    and our lives shared in common.

May the peace, and the love, and the blessing of God
    always rest upon our table.
Alleluia! Amen!

(Adapted from
Prayers for the Domestic Church)

Third Sunday of Easter

"Have You Anything Here to Eat?"

Scripture

- *Acts 3:13–19.* Let us repent and turn away from sinfulness.
- *1 John 2:1–5.* Do not sin. But if you do, Jesus is your advocate.
- *Luke 24:35–48.* Jesus eats and then asks that repentance be preached in his name.

Theme

It is such a struggle to turn away from sin. Jesus knows that. We try to follow his ways, but we sometimes fail. And we are deeply troubled. That is where repentance and forgiveness come in. They are as basic to our needs as food. And Jesus is concerned with both when he asks, "Why are you troubled, and have you anything to eat?"

Focusing Object
A dinner plate

Reflections

For Adults

When standing face-to-face with Jesus, his disciples, despite their joy in seeing him, were confused and in shock. He asked them why they were troubled, and why questions were rising in their hearts?

- When you are troubled, what is it that usually troubles you? When questions rise in your heart, what are they? Why do they bother you?

Jesus might have had two reasons for asking about food. He might have wanted to calm down his friends and prove to them that he was not a ghost because ghosts do not eat. But he also might have just wanted the company and familiarity of sharing a meal with his friends.

- When has eating calmed your fears? When has sharing a meal with friends made you feel better? What was one of the best meals you ever had? Who was there?

For Teenagers

Jesus shows up at a gathering of friends, and the first thing he does is ask what might be troubling them, and whether there is anything to eat. Eating is an important part of sharing time with friends. Who would ever think of having a party without having food? Jesus knew how important sharing food with friends is.

- Describe one of the best times you had sharing food with your best friends.
- When Jesus appeared, his friends were shocked. They felt joy, fear, confusion, and disbelief all rolled up together. It was too good to be true. Did you ever experience anything that was too good to be true? What happened? How did you and your friends, or your family, react? What did you do to celebrate?

For Children

- If Jesus showed up at your house and asked whether you had anything there to eat, what would you give him?
- Jesus loved to eat and party with his friends. If you could have a party and invite some of your friends, who would you invite? What food would you want to eat?
- Do you like to cook? Have you helped cook a meal? What foods would you like to cook?

Closing

Be present at our table, Lord.
Be here and everywhere adored.
Thy creatures bless and grant that we
May feast in Paradise with Thee.
John Cennick (1718–1755)
(One Hundred Graces)

Third Sunday of Easter

26 April 1998
29 April 2001
25 April 2004

"Have You Caught Any Fish?"

Scripture

- *Acts 5:27–32,40–41.* The Apostles ignored the warning not to preach about Jesus.
- *Revelation 5:11–14.* John had a vision of thousands of voices praising Jesus.
- ○ *John 21:1–19.* Jesus sees the Apostles fishing; he prepares a breakfast of cooked fish.

Theme

The Apostles recognized Jesus when he told them to cast their empty net on the other side of the boat and it was filled. Jesus was already cooking fish on a fire—he anticipated their needs and was ready to minister to them. He later made Peter assure him three times that he would take care of the followers. Sure enough, Peter and the Apostles kept preaching despite the warnings to stop. John had a vision of what the Holy Spirit could bring about.

Focusing Object
A mounted fish or a picture of a fish

Reflections

For Adults

- The Apostles were as filled with the Spirit as their nets had been filled with fish. Have you ever felt such courage and spirit that you continued to do God's work, despite warnings to stop? Where did that feeling come from? Share your experience of being filled with the Spirit.

155

- Many of the Apostles had been fishermen. Have you ever been fishing? Do you enjoy it? Why or why not? Why is it significant that we hear stories about the Apostles being unsuccessful at catching fish until Jesus has them lower their nets on the other side of the boat?
- Jesus asking Peter three times to feed his lambs parallels the three times Peter denied Jesus the night Jesus was arrested. Have you ever treated someone badly, been forgiven, and then been asked to do that person a favor? What happened? How did it feel?

For Teenagers

- Have you ever been fishing? If so, did you enjoy it? If not, do you think you would enjoy it? What would you say are the biggest challenges of fishing? What is most frustrating about it? What is most rewarding?
- If you were fishing on one side of the boat and you were not catching any fish, would you follow someone's suggestion to switch sides? Do you think that could help? Jesus had the disciples do this more than once in the Gospel stories. Why do you think he told them to do that? Why do you think they listened to him?
- The Apostles became courageously loyal to Jesus. Eventually, most of them were martyred. How would you explain such conviction? Is there anything or anyone you could feel that loyal to? Why or why not? What would you be willing to do for that person or that cause?

For Children

- Have you ever gone fishing? If so, what was it like? Did you enjoy it? Did you catch any fish? Did you cook and eat them? What is the best part of fishing? What is the worst part of it? If you have never gone fishing, would you like to? What do you think you might like or dislike about it? Do you like the taste of fish?

When the Apostles were out fishing they often took most of their clothes off because it was hot and wet on the boats. When they were finished they put their clothes back on. But Peter became really excited when he saw Jesus. He got so mixed up, he did something silly—he put his clothes back on, and then he jumped into the water!

• Have you ever been so excited that you did something silly like that? What happened?

Closing

Dear God, be good to me.
The sea is so wide,
And my boat is so small.
   (From France, Breton fisherman's prayer)

Lord, what a blessing is the sea
with fish in plenty.
   (From Ghana, a fisherman's prayer)

Be gracious to me, my Father,
hold up my boat.
   (From South America, Andean Yahgan people)

(Peace on Earth)

Fourth Sunday of Easter

28 April 1996
25 April 1999
21 April 2002

The Sheepgate

Scripture

- *Acts 2:14,36–41.* Baptism and the Holy Spirit will keep us from going astray.
- *1 Peter 2:20–25.* We have returned to the shepherd and guardian of our souls.
- ○ *John 10:1–10.* Jesus is the sheepgate, the door; enter through him and be saved.

Theme

We do not want to stray from the fold, we want to be with our shepherd and guardian. Only shepherds enter through the sheepgate; true shepherds come by way of Jesus, call us forth, and lead us in right paths. Those who would call to us and lead us that do not come by way of Jesus are thieves and robbers, leading us astray.

Focusing Object
A figure of a sheep, or a wool scarf, wool socks, or the like

Reflections

For Adults

Sheep are not very bright animals. Once they get going, they will follow each other anywhere. It is easy to lead them astray. That is why they need a good shepherd they are familiar with. Being compared to sheep isn't exactly complimentary, but it is accurate in some ways. Get some people going, and they will follow one another anywhere.

- Have you ever followed someone who led you astray? How were you fooled? What did you learn from your experience?
- Jesus has come so we might have life and have it to the full. How is your life changed when you take that message seriously?

For Teenagers

Jesus is the front door. Anyone else sneaking around, climbing fences, going through the back door, or doing anything in secret means trouble. Be up-front, do what you do in broad daylight, and it is usually the right thing. You are proud of what you do when it is the right thing. If you are sneaking because you do not want to get caught, you are probably doing something wrong! Doing the right thing brings abundant life! Doing wrong things can hurt your ability to enjoy life abundantly.

- What is "abundant life" or "life to the full"? Do you think you can get it through Jesus? Do you think you can get it sneaking around, trying back doors, and climbing over fences? Why or why not?

Sheep pretty much follow the crowd. Not too many sheep are "individuals." Being an individual is fine, especially when the crowd is not a good bunch to follow. But following the crowd can be fine too, especially when the crowd is a fine crowd and is doing good things.

- Are you usually an individual? Or do you prefer to follow the crowd? Give an example of when you have been either an individual or a crowd follower.
- How can you tell if someone who wants you to follow them is really following the way of Jesus?

For Children

- Have you ever seen a sheep at a farm or a zoo? Did you ever pet a sheep? What does it feel like? Do you like the way it feels?
- We get wool from sheep. Do you have anything that is made from wool? If so, do you like wearing it or using it? Is it soft or scratchy?

- A shepherd is the one who takes care of sheep. We need Jesus in the same way sheep need a shepherd. Knowing about Jesus and praying to Jesus is what keeps us doing the right things. What have you learned about Jesus? What kind of things does Jesus like you to do?

Closing

Jesus liked to tell stories about nature. To get his point across, he often chose themes people could relate to, and everyone can relate to stories of nature. That is why so many stories involve rocks, seeds, vines, branches, trees, and sheep.

O' Great Spirit,
Whose voice I hear in the winds,
And whose breath gives life to all the world,
hear me!
I am small and weak, I need your
strength and wisdom.

Let me walk in beauty, and make my eyes
ever behold the red and purple sunset.

Make my hands respect the things you have
made and my ears sharp to hear your voice.

Make me wise so that I may understand the
things you have taught my people.

Let me learn the lessons you have hidden
in every leaf and rock.

I seek strength, not to be greater than my
brother, but to fight my greatest
enemy—myself.

Make me always ready to come to you with
clean hands and straight eyes.

So when life fades, as the fading sunset,
my spirit may come to you
without shame.

("An Indian Prayer," a Lakota prayer)

Fourth Sunday of Easter

20 April 1997
14 May 2000
11 May 2003

The Good Shepherd

Scripture

- *Acts 4:8–12.* The stone rejected by the builders has become the cornerstone.
- *1 John 3:1–2.* We are God's children.
- *John 10:11–18.* I am the Good Shepherd.

Theme

God loves all of us. We are all God's children. Even the rejected stones can be cornerstones in building God's Kingdom. Jesus is the good shepherd who knows his sheep and cares deeply for all of them. He lays his life down for all of us, even the most rejected ones.

Focusing Object
A cowboy hat, toy tractor, or small toy sheep, horse, or cow

Reflections

For Adults

The one who owns and cares for the sheep is different from the one who is hired to watch them. The first has ownership and investment. The second is going through the motions for the payoff.
- In what areas of your life might you be just going through the motions?
- In what areas do you have real ownership and investment?
- Is there something or someone you would lay down your life for?

161

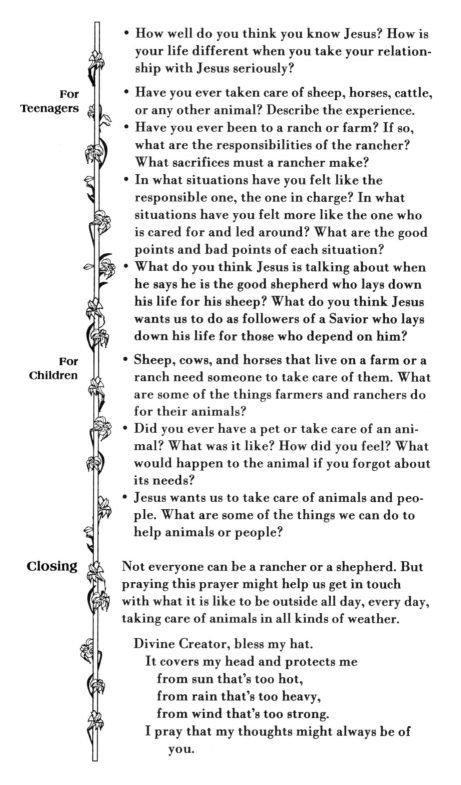

- How well do you think you know Jesus? How is your life different when you take your relationship with Jesus seriously?

For Teenagers

- Have you ever taken care of sheep, horses, cattle, or any other animal? Describe the experience.
- Have you ever been to a ranch or farm? If so, what are the responsibilities of the rancher? What sacrifices must a rancher make?
- In what situations have you felt like the responsible one, the one in charge? In what situations have you felt more like the one who is cared for and led around? What are the good points and bad points of each situation?
- What do you think Jesus is talking about when he says he is the good shepherd who lays down his life for his sheep? What do you think Jesus wants us to do as followers of a Savior who lays down his life for those who depend on him?

For Children

- Sheep, cows, and horses that live on a farm or a ranch need someone to take care of them. What are some of the things farmers and ranchers do for their animals?
- Did you ever have a pet or take care of an animal? What was it like? How did you feel? What would happen to the animal if you forgot about its needs?
- Jesus wants us to take care of animals and people. What are some of the things we can do to help animals or people?

Closing

Not everyone can be a rancher or a shepherd. But praying this prayer might help us get in touch with what it is like to be outside all day, every day, taking care of animals in all kinds of weather.

Divine Creator, bless my hat.
  It covers my head and protects me
    from sun that's too hot,
    from rain that's too heavy,
    from wind that's too strong.
  I pray that my thoughts might always be of
    you.

Almighty Creator, bless my boots.
　　They protect my feet and keep me going
　　　　over ground that is rocky,
　　　　on fields that are muddy and slippery,
　　　　over hills and bluffs that are steep.
　　I pray that I might always follow your path.
Loving Creator, bless my horse, my cattle, and
　　　　my sheep.
　　They involuntarily give their lives
　　　　in service to my work
　　　　and my livelihood.
　　I pray that I might never take my blessings
　　　　for granted.
　　　　　　　　　　Amen.
　　　　　　　　　　　　("Rancher's Prayer")

Fourth Sunday of Easter

C

3 May 1998
6 May 2001
2 May 2004

God Will Wipe Away Every Tear

Scripture

- *Acts 13:14,43–52.* As Paul traveled to preach, many believed, but some disapproved.
- *Revelation 7:9,14–17.* John saw a vision of people joined with God and suffering no more.
- *John 10:27–30.* Those who follow Jesus and the One who sent him will never perish.

Theme

Paul and his company were not discouraged when the religious authorities stirred up persecution against them. They were joyful for the followers they gained. Jesus promises eternal life to those who follow him. John's vision is one of comfort—the followers have no more hunger, no more thirst, no more scorching heat, and no more tears.

Focusing Object
A hanky or tissue

Reflections

For Adults

- What are some of the sufferings you have witnessed or experienced in your adult life that have brought you to tears? How did you come to be comforted eventually?
- How can we bring comfort to those around us who suffer? What could bring some real solutions to the problems of poverty, unemploy-

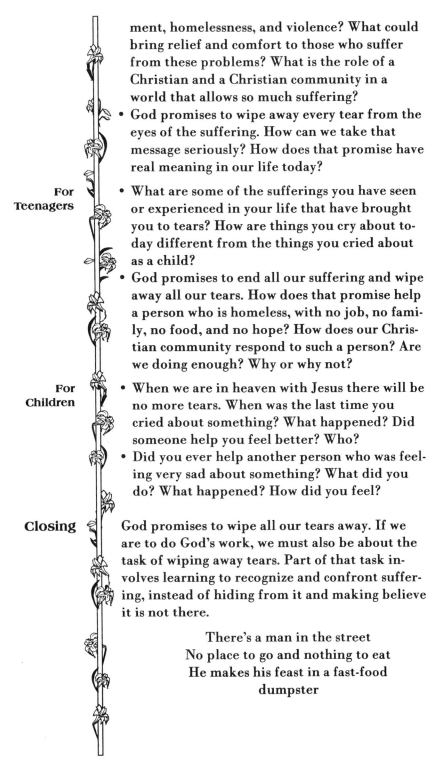

ment, homelessness, and violence? What could bring relief and comfort to those who suffer from these problems? What is the role of a Christian and a Christian community in a world that allows so much suffering?

- God promises to wipe away every tear from the eyes of the suffering. How can we take that message seriously? How does that promise have real meaning in our life today?

For Teenagers

- What are some of the sufferings you have seen or experienced in your life that have brought you to tears? How are things you cry about to-day different from the things you cried about as a child?
- God promises to end all our suffering and wipe away all our tears. How does that promise help a person who is homeless, with no job, no family, no food, and no hope? How does our Christian community respond to such a person? Are we doing enough? Why or why not?

For Children

- When we are in heaven with Jesus there will be no more tears. When was the last time you cried about something? What happened? Did someone help you feel better? Who?
- Did you ever help another person who was feeling very sad about something? What did you do? What happened? How did you feel?

Closing

God promises to wipe all our tears away. If we are to do God's work, we must also be about the task of wiping away tears. Part of that task involves learning to recognize and confront suffering, instead of hiding from it and making believe it is not there.

There's a man in the street
No place to go and nothing to eat
He makes his feast in a fast-food
dumpster

Fries, Chicken, Bread, and Rolls
tossed amidst the everyday trash
The man hangs his head low
His shoulders drop
feet shuffle forth
No place to go
No place to call home
He rests his body on the
warm stenchy sewer vents
Clenching his shoes in a fetal position
The weather worn face
Hides the child he once was
and the man he strives to be.
(Kelly Milbourn, a high school student)

Fifth Sunday of Easter

Service

Scripture

○ *Acts 6:1–7.* Seven deacons are appointed to help serve the community's needs.
• *1 Peter 2:4–9.* The stone (Jesus) rejected by the builders has become the cornerstone.
• *John 14:1–12.* Jesus is the way, the truth, and the life.

Theme

Jesus' whole life was about service. Since Jesus is the way, the truth, and the life, service is the way to truth and to life. In fact, service as a lifestyle is often rejected as being demeaning and beneath dignity, yet a life of service has become the cornerstone of our faith. The early Christians knew this. They appointed Stephen and six others to concentrate on service to the community's needs.

Focusing Object
A sandal

Reflections

For Adults

• What do you think of when you hear the word *service?* Do you think of military service? service in a restaurant? a paid servant, like a butler? mission work in a foreign country? Do most people in our country believe in everyday service as a lifestyle, no matter what their occupation or career is? Why or why not?

Christian service is often talked about as having two "feet." Each has to be used if we are to take any steps and walk forward successfully. One "foot" is direct services to people in need. This includes anything done to get food to the hungry, to provide shelter to the homeless, to care for the sick, and the like. The other "foot" is work aimed at changing the structures that cause the problems in the first place, such as writing letters, changing laws, educating, and so forth. In other words, the first foot is giving a hungry person a fish to eat; the second foot is teaching hungry people how to fish so they can get themselves something to eat.

- What agencies are available in your area to serve each of these needs? How have you been involved in the past? What can be done to encourage wider involvement in service?

For Teenagers

- "Nice guys finish last." "Look out for number 1." "Be the 'me' generation." Have you ever heard these sayings? What kind of lifestyle do they promote? Why do you think they became popular? Can a person really live an active Christian lifestyle without opposing this philosophy of life? Why or why not?
- What do you think are the most important things in life? What does society, the mainstream culture in our country, say are the most important things in life? What does Jesus say are the most important things in life? How does all that relate to service?
- The sandal is a symbol of service. How and why do you think a sandal symbolizes service?

For Children

The church had a lot of needs when it was getting started. Everyone got together to help one another so everyone had food, everyone had clothing, everyone had a place to live, and everyone could be taught about Jesus. Some people were deacons, and it was their job to be sure everyone was taken care of. They helped everyone get what they needed.

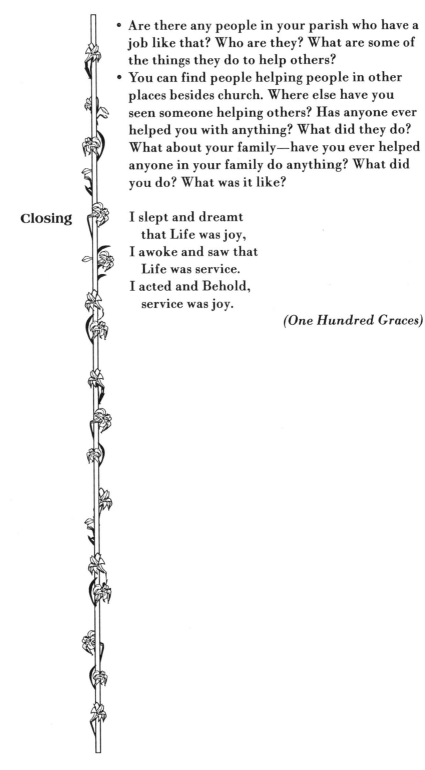

- Are there any people in your parish who have a job like that? Who are they? What are some of the things they do to help others?
- You can find people helping people in other places besides church. Where else have you seen someone helping others? Has anyone ever helped you with anything? What did they do? What about your family—have you ever helped anyone in your family do anything? What did you do? What was it like?

Closing

I slept and dreamt
  that Life was joy,
I awoke and saw that
  Life was service.
I acted and Behold,
  service was joy.

(One Hundred Graces)

Fifth Sunday of Easter

27 April 1997
21 May 2000
18 May 2003

The Vine and the Branches

Scripture

- *Acts 9:26–31.* Paul begins preaching about Jesus.
- *1 John 3:18–24.* We need to believe in Jesus and to love one another.
- *John 15:1–8.* Jesus is the vine and we are the branches.

Theme

We cannot do much good without Jesus. All that is good, all that is healthy, all that is right comes from Jesus, as does our very life. Branches have no life apart from the vine. That means we need to believe in all he stands for, to love one another, and to live our lives abiding in him and in all his words.

Focusing Object
A plant with branches

Reflections

For Adults

Our connection to Jesus is as simple as the connection of vine and branches. Jesus is our lifeline. The time we are most conscious of Jesus in our life is the time we are most likely to do our best work—to bear fruit.

- Think back to a time when you accomplished something worthwhile. How was Jesus active in your life at that time? What was happening?

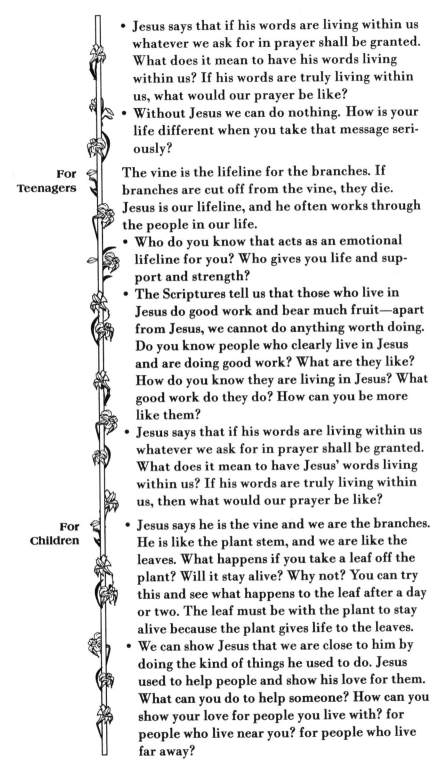

- Jesus says that if his words are living within us whatever we ask for in prayer shall be granted. What does it mean to have his words living within us? If his words are truly living within us, what would our prayer be like?
- Without Jesus we can do nothing. How is your life different when you take that message seriously?

For Teenagers

The vine is the lifeline for the branches. If branches are cut off from the vine, they die. Jesus is our lifeline, and he often works through the people in our life.

- Who do you know that acts as an emotional lifeline for you? Who gives you life and support and strength?
- The Scriptures tell us that those who live in Jesus do good work and bear much fruit—apart from Jesus, we cannot do anything worth doing. Do you know people who clearly live in Jesus and are doing good work? What are they like? How do you know they are living in Jesus? What good work do they do? How can you be more like them?
- Jesus says that if his words are living within us whatever we ask for in prayer shall be granted. What does it mean to have Jesus' words living within us? If his words are truly living within us, then what would our prayer be like?

For Children

- Jesus says he is the vine and we are the branches. He is like the plant stem, and we are like the leaves. What happens if you take a leaf off the plant? Will it stay alive? Why not? You can try this and see what happens to the leaf after a day or two. The leaf must be with the plant to stay alive because the plant gives life to the leaves.
- We can show Jesus that we are close to him by doing the kind of things he used to do. Jesus used to help people and show his love for them. What can you do to help someone? How can you show your love for people you live with? for people who live near you? for people who live far away?

Closing

O God, who taught Adam and Eve the simple
art of tilling the soil,
You sent us Jesus Christ, the true vine,
So we could always be rooted to you in love.
We pray
That we might follow the example
Of Isidore and his wife Maria,
So that our hearts cultivate a horror of sin and
a love for prayer.
May we learn
To work the soil with the sweat of our brow
And to follow the ways of your Spirit
So we might enjoy eternal happiness in heaven
with you. Amen.

(Adapted from "Prayer in Honor of Saint
Isidore")

Fifth Sunday of Easter

10 May 1998
13 May 2001
9 May 2004

A New
Heaven and
a New Earth

Scripture

- *Acts 14:21–27.* Paul and Barnabas travel great distances preaching to the Gentiles.
- *Revelation 21:1–5.* John has a vision of a new heaven, a new earth, and a new Jerusalem.
- *John 13:31–35.* Jesus commands us to love one another.

Theme

It is fascinating to think about how big the world is, and yet how small the earth is. In Paul's day, travel was a lot more difficult, and still he and others managed to journey across all of the known earth, preaching to the Gentiles. John has a vision of a new heaven and a new earth— a peaceful place with no pain and no problems, not even death. Jesus tells us what brings heaven to earth: love, the global universal value.

Focusing Object
A globe or a world map

Reflections

For Adults

Like the song in one of Disney World's attractions says, "It's a small world after all." Modern transportation and communication connect points all over the globe in a way never imagined by Paul.
- What kind of experiences remind you that it is a safe, neighborly, and small world? What

experiences remind you that the world is still huge and frightening? When you imagine "a new heaven and a new earth," what is it like? How is it better?

• Have you ever traveled to another continent? If so, what was your travel like? How did you view the cultures you were able to visit? What could we learn from those cultures? Where else would you like to travel and why? If you haven't ever traveled beyond this continent, would you like to? Where would you like to visit? What would you like to experience? Why?

For Teenagers

• What is really good about our world? What is not so good? If you could help create the "new heaven and the new earth," what would you want the design to include?

• Why do you think so many schools require students to learn a foreign language? Why do you think countries have exchange student programs? How can we learn from visiting one another's countries, and from having citizens from other countries visit ours? What can different languages and cultures teach us?

• Love seems to be a universal value in all cultures. All cultures celebrate marriage, children, family life, and friendship based on love and caring. If this is true, why is there so much friction between peoples of different countries and different races?

For Children

• How many countries on the earth can you name? Would you like to visit any of them? Why or why not? What do you think the people would be like in different countries?

• Do you know any words in a different language?

• Let's pretend God was going to create a new heaven and a new earth, and God was asking you for some advice on how to do a better job. What things would you tell God to make better? What are some of the problems with our earth that you think God would like to have fixed?

Closing

Blessed is the spot, and the house,
and the place, and the city,

and the heart, and the mountain,
and the refuge, and the cave,
and the valley, and the land,

and the sea and the island
and the meadow where mention
of God hath been made,

and [God's] praise glorified.

(*Peace on Earth*, an Iranian prayer
from the Bahá'í faith tradition)

Sixth Sunday of Easter

12 May 1996
9 May 1999
5 May 2002

The Spirit Will Be Sent

Scripture

○ *Acts 8:5–8,14–17.* They are baptized, they have hands laid on them, and they receive the Spirit.
• *1 Peter 3:15–18.* We are to honor and reverence Jesus in our hearts.
• *John 14:15–21.* We are to keep Jesus' commandments; the Spirit will be sent to us.

Theme

Jesus came to teach us the way of God. Jesus promised us the Spirit—the Spirit of Yahweh, the Spirit of Jesus, the Spirit that is alive in all of us. When we honor Jesus in our hearts and our actions, we are following the way he taught us to live, and the Spirit is alive and acting through us.

Focusing Object
An image of a dove

Reflections

For Adults

Jesus' commandments are very simple: Take care of the little ones; love God; love one another; serve one another; believe. When these simple commands are not followed, the world's major problems erupt. When they are being followed, it is the Holy Spirit at work in us.
• When do you let the Holy Spirit work in you? How has the Holy Spirit worked in you? What

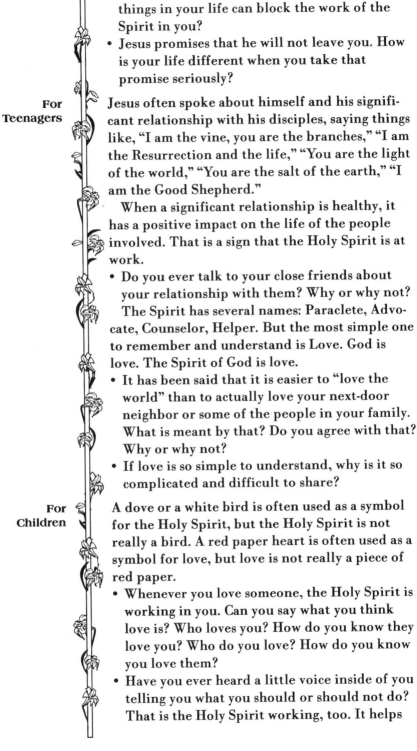

things in your life can block the work of the Spirit in you?

- Jesus promises that he will not leave you. How is your life different when you take that promise seriously?

For Teenagers

Jesus often spoke about himself and his significant relationship with his disciples, saying things like, "I am the vine, you are the branches," "I am the Resurrection and the life," "You are the light of the world," "You are the salt of the earth," "I am the Good Shepherd."

When a significant relationship is healthy, it has a positive impact on the life of the people involved. That is a sign that the Holy Spirit is at work.

- Do you ever talk to your close friends about your relationship with them? Why or why not?

The Spirit has several names: Paraclete, Advocate, Counselor, Helper. But the most simple one to remember and understand is Love. God is love. The Spirit of God is love.

- It has been said that it is easier to "love the world" than to actually love your next-door neighbor or some of the people in your family. What is meant by that? Do you agree with that? Why or why not?

- If love is so simple to understand, why is it so complicated and difficult to share?

For Children

A dove or a white bird is often used as a symbol for the Holy Spirit, but the Holy Spirit is not really a bird. A red paper heart is often used as a symbol for love, but love is not really a piece of red paper.

- Whenever you love someone, the Holy Spirit is working in you. Can you say what you think love is? Who loves you? How do you know they love you? Who do you love? How do you know you love them?

- Have you ever heard a little voice inside of you telling you what you should or should not do? That is the Holy Spirit working, too. It helps

you do the right things. When we do good things, we feel good inside. When was a time you felt good about something you did? When we do bad things, we feel bad inside. When was a time you felt bad about something you did?

Closing

'Tis a gift to be simple,
'Tis a gift to be free;
'Tis a gift to come down
   where we ought to be.
And when we find ourselves in the place
   just right,
'Twill be in the valley
   of love and delight.

When true simplicity is gained,
To bow and to bend
   We will not be ashamed.
To turn, turn,
   will be our delight,
'Till by turning, turning
   we come round right.

("Simple Gifts," a traditional Shaker song)

Sixth Sunday of Easter

4 May 1997
28 May 2000
25 May 2003

The God of Every Nation

Scripture

- ○ *Acts 10:25–26,34–35,44–48.* God shows no partiality of nations.
- • *1 John 4:7–10.* Let us love one another, because love is of God.
- • *John 15:9–17.* Love one another as I have loved you.

Theme

In every nation, the people who love are doing the work of God. No one country is better than another. We are called to love each other regardless of which nation we call home.

Focusing Object
A flag or symbol from the United States or from any other nation

Reflections

For Adults

The Jews had always believed that they were the chosen people, and that Gentiles (people who were not Jewish) were less worthy and less human. It took the miracle of the Holy Spirit being showered on Jews and Gentiles alike for Peter to realize that being the chosen people did not mean being the superior people. It still took a while for Jews to accept Gentiles as equals in this new community of believers. It is easy to say we are all equal; much harder to actually live that belief.

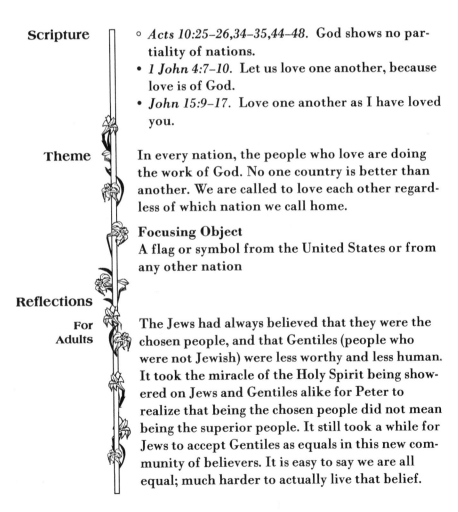

179

The United States of America can learn a lot from Peter. This country, supposedly built on freedom, prospered because people who arrived on the shores thought themselves superior to the natives already living here and to the Africans they kidnapped to use as slaves.

- How many friends do you have of different races? How do you perceive people who are Native American? African American? Hispanic American? Asian American? European American?
- What is a racist? Do you think racism is a sin?
- How do you perceive people from the Deep South? people from up North? people on the East Coast? on the West Coast? How do you perceive men? women? people who live in inner cities? people who live in suburbs? people who live in rural farm areas? homeless people? Is there anyone you feel superior to?
- The Scriptures say that God shows no partiality. How is your life different when you take that message seriously?

For Teenagers

Gang-related violence is becoming a concern all over. In Jesus' and Peter's world, the two big "gangs" were the Jews and the Gentiles. Jesus started building bridges between the two groups, and Peter and the other disciples continued the work. At first, it was difficult for most Jews who grew up thinking themselves superior to Gentiles to live with them as equals and as friends.

- Is there a group of people you feel superior to? a group you feel inferior to? How many friends do you have who are Native American? African American? Hispanic American? Asian American? European American?
- Is there racial tension where you live and attend school? In the United States, everyone is supposed to be treated equally. Do you believe this is what happens? Why or why not?
- Gangs are not formed only along racial lines. Gangs or cliques can form in any community.

Sometimes athletes associate only with other athletes; sometimes actors and musicians hang out together; sometimes people with high incomes socialize only with people in the same income bracket. Are there cliques in your school? Are some groups seen as superior to others? What is the social structure? Why do you think it exists? What can be done about it?

For Children

- Jesus loved everyone and had a lot of friends. But some people still did not like Jesus. Do you know anyone who does not like you? How does that make you feel? Why do you think they don't like you?
- Is there anyone you know that you don't like? Why don't you like them? Sometimes there are good reasons for staying away from a person and not liking them. But some reasons are silly. Do you think your reasons are good reasons or silly ones?

Closing

Martin Luther King, Jr., knew the pain of racism. He became the pastor of Dexter Avenue Baptist Church in Montgomery, Alabama, in 1954, and spent his life promoting civil rights. King said, "Injustice anywhere is a threat to justice everywhere." In Memphis, Tennessee, on April 4, 1968, he was shot and killed. Excerpts from his most famous speech, made on August 28, 1963, at the Lincoln Memorial in Washington, D.C., follow.

"I have a dream that one day this nation will rise up and live out the true meaning of its creed: 'We hold these truths to be self-evident; that all men are created equal.' . . .

"I have a dream that my four little children will one day live in a nation where they will not be judged by the color of their skin but by the content of their character. . . .

"And if America is to be a great nation, this must become true. . . .

"When we let freedom ring, when we let it ring from every village and every hamlet, from every state and every city, we will be able to speed up that day when all of God's children, black men and white men, Jews and Gentiles, Protestants and Catholics, will be able to join hands and sing in the words of the old Negro spiritual, 'Free at last! Free at last! Thank God Almighty, we are free at last!'"

(The SCLC Story in Words and Pictures)

Sixth Sunday of Easter

C

17 May 1998
20 May 2001
16 May 2004

The Glory
of God Is
Our Light,
Our Lamp Is
the Lamb

Scripture

- *Acts 15:1–2,22–29.* It was decided that the circumcision of Gentiles was not necessary.
- *Revelation 21:10–14,22–23.* The only light needed for the city was from God.
- *John 14:23–29.* Jesus comforts and promises that the Spirit will come to teach and enlighten.

Theme

Lamps have always been a symbol of learning, with the light from the lamp representing our own enlightenment. Jesus promises us that the Spirit will come to teach the Apostles. At the Council of Jerusalem, many disciples gathered to enlighten one another about how the Gentiles received the gift of the Holy Spirit without first being circumcised. And John's great vision reminds us that the only lamp we need is the Lamb of God—one of Jesus' titles.

Focusing Object
A lamp

Reflections

**For
Adults**

If Jesus is our lamp, and the light is the glory of God, then learning from Jesus is our way to bring glory to God and enlightenment to ourselves and others. Whenever people pray together and are open to the Spirit, they are enlightened.

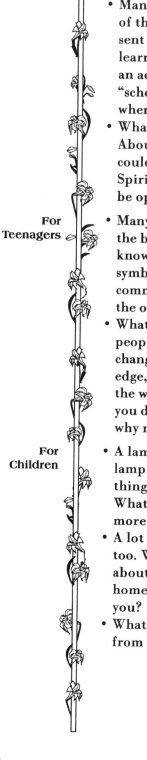

- Many colleges and universities use the symbol of the burning oil lamp on their seals to represent knowledge. Share one of your significant learning experiences—whether it occurred in an actual institution of learning or in the "school of life." What happened to your life when you applied this learning experience?
- What areas in your life need enlightenment? About what issues do you wish learned people could gather, pray, discuss, and be open to the Spirit? To what area of learning do you need to be open?

For Teenagers

- Many colleges and universities use the symbol of the burning oil lamp on their seal to represent knowledge. Why do you think that is a natural symbol? What do light and knowledge have in common? How is Jesus like a lamp? What might the oil—the fuel used for light—represent?
- What do you think the world needs more of— people willing to learn, or people willing to change things? Is it harder to learn, gain knowledge, and propose solutions, or is it harder to do the work, take action, and create change? Can you do one without doing the other? Why or why not? Where might you fit in?

For Children

- A lamp is a symbol of learning. School is like a lamp that helps us to learn. We can learn many things with school as our lamp for learning. What are some things you would like to learn more about in school?
- A lot of learning takes place outside school, too. What kind of things have you learned about outside of school? What did you learn at home? What things has your family taught you?
- What has Jesus taught us? What can we learn from the church?

Closing

This poem to the six high powers was traditionally spoken every morning by the Omaha people. Seeking knowledge and guidance from the divine is a traditional action present in many different cultures.

Sun upon high—power over all—show yourself
    on your seat.
I pray that you will understand that whatever I
    do,
  I desire only good.
Moon, there on high, have pity on me;
  give me the good road.
Pity and help me; whatever I do,
  I desire only the good.
Sky-father above: you, seated there.
I pray you to understand that whatever I do,
  I desire only good.
Earth, there, I pray you, Mother.
Pity me. Good is what I desire.
Winds of the four quarters: give me the good
    road.
Whatever I do, I desire good.
Rock, old grandfather seated there, remaining
    firmly seated,
Keep me firm and straight.

                   ("The Omaha Creation Hymn")

Seventh Sunday of Easter

19 May 1996
16 May 1999
12 May 2002

Prayer

Scripture

- *Acts 1:12–14.* The Apostles and the women with them devoted themselves to prayer.
- *1 Peter 4:13–16.* The Spirit of God, the Spirit of Glory, rests upon us.
- *John 17:1–11.* Jesus prays for his followers.

Theme

We read in the Scriptures how devoted the followers of Jesus were to prayer. Jesus himself was very devoted to prayer. He used to escape to a place where he could be alone and pray. Jesus prayed for his followers. He prayed for us. Prayer is divine communication with God.

Focusing Object
A prayer book

Reflections

For Adults

- Jesus said eternal life was knowing the one true God. Are you reasonably certain that you know the one true God? Who is God for you? Why do you believe in God? How did you come to believe in God?
- Jesus and his followers were devoted to prayer. In what ways do you pray? Is your prayer more of a one-way conversation, or a two-way conversation? How does God speak to you?

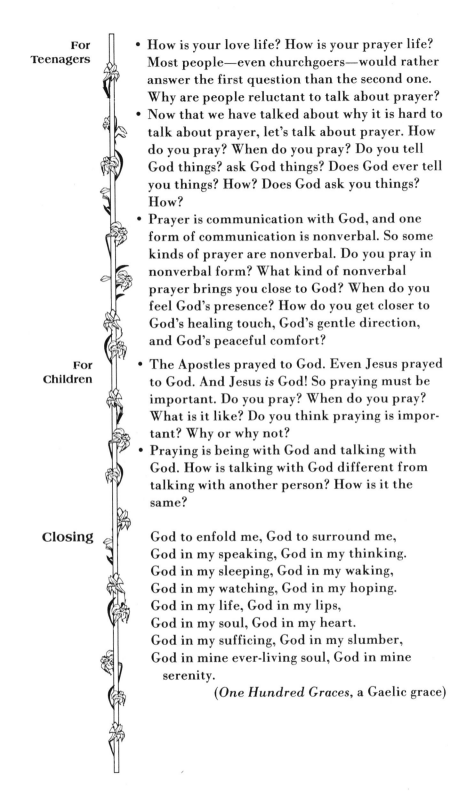

For Teenagers

- How is your love life? How is your prayer life? Most people—even churchgoers—would rather answer the first question than the second one. Why are people reluctant to talk about prayer?
- Now that we have talked about why it is hard to talk about prayer, let's talk about prayer. How do you pray? When do you pray? Do you tell God things? ask God things? Does God ever tell you things? How? Does God ask you things? How?
- Prayer is communication with God, and one form of communication is nonverbal. So some kinds of prayer are nonverbal. Do you pray in nonverbal form? What kind of nonverbal prayer brings you close to God? When do you feel God's presence? How do you get closer to God's healing touch, God's gentle direction, and God's peaceful comfort?

For Children

- The Apostles prayed to God. Even Jesus prayed to God. And Jesus *is* God! So praying must be important. Do you pray? When do you pray? What is it like? Do you think praying is important? Why or why not?
- Praying is being with God and talking with God. How is talking with God different from talking with another person? How is it the same?

Closing

God to enfold me, God to surround me,
God in my speaking, God in my thinking.
God in my sleeping, God in my waking,
God in my watching, God in my hoping.
God in my life, God in my lips,
God in my soul, God in my heart.
God in my sufficing, God in my slumber,
God in mine ever-living soul, God in mine
    serenity.

               (*One Hundred Graces*, a Gaelic grace)

Seventh Sunday of Easter

11 May 1997
4 June 2000
1 June 2003

The Luck of the Spirit

Scripture

○ *Acts 1:15–17,20–26.* Matthias was chosen to replace Judas by casting lots.
• *1 John 4:11–16.* We know and believe because we have been given God's own Spirit.
• *John 17:11–19.* Like Jesus, we are in this world, but we are not of this world.

Theme

Although we live *in* this world, we need to know that we are not *of* this world. We are of the world beyond this world, the world of the Spirit, which we cannot see or touch, but which we know and believe. In the world of the Spirit, we have the confidence to pray, to cast lots, and to accept what happens. We can trust the luck of the Spirit.

Focusing Object
A deck of playing cards or a pair of dice

Reflections

For Adults

When the Apostles wanted to replace Judas, they had a certain requirement—the candidates had to have been with Jesus from the baptism of John up until the time of the Ascension. They called forth only two that could meet the requirement—Barsabbas and Matthias. They did not vote. They did not have a competition. They merely prayed, trusted the Spirit, and cast lots.

• What do you think about praying, trusting the Spirit, and casting lots? If you were a company president, would you use that system in trying to decide which of two job applicants you should hire? Why or why not? If you were applying for a job, would you be willing to go through that system as your hiring procedure? Why or why not? When would you trust that system? Why was it a good choice for the Apostles?

Matthias won by the luck of the Spirit, as well as the luck of the draw. But what did he win? An easy job and an easy life? Or a challenging life that included hardship, danger, and sacrifice?

• Have you ever won a mixed blessing? Were you ever lucky enough to be chosen for something difficult and full of sacrifice? How did you feel at the time? How do you feel about it now?

For Teenagers

The Apostles had to pick between Matthias and Barsabbas. They did not have a contest or a vote. They prayed, trusted the Spirit, and cast lots. Casting lots is like tossing dice or drawing cards. Matthias won.

• If you were Matthias, would you feel as if you really won? Or would you have preferred a real competition that would have demonstrated who the best candidate truly was? If you were Barsabbas, would you have felt it was a fair contest, or would you have felt cheated? Why or why not?

People who are more competitive might prefer a contest, but less-competitive people might prefer the casting of lots because the gifts and qualifications of both candidates were affirmed. In trusting the luck of the Spirit, there is no one to blame for a choice that seems disagreeable.

• Do you see advantages and disadvantages to the luck of the Spirit? Are you more of a competitive type of person or a cooperative person? What does the Apostles' method of making a choice say about the kind of people they were? Is there something we can learn from that?

- Do you think you are unlucky or lucky? Do you believe that a person can actually be lucky or unlucky? Do you think people can create their own luck? Explain your answers.

For Children

- Do you know any games that use dice or cards? What are they? Do you like to play them? Do you usually win or lose? Or do you win some and lose some? Do you think you are a lucky person? Why or why not?

When Jesus' Apostles were trying to pick a new Apostle, first they prayed to pick the right person, then they did something called casting lots. Casting lots is like tossing dice or playing cards. The person who got picked was Matthias.

- Does your family or class ever toss dice or draw cards or straws in order to pick someone for something? Do you think that is a good idea?

Closing

O God who knows the hearts of all,
  You bless us with good luck and bad luck.
  Sometimes an ace is lucky, sometimes it is
    unlucky.
  Sometimes we toss the dice and we win a
    wonderful prize.
  Sometimes we toss the dice and what we win
    is a mixed blessing.

Help us to praise the luck of the Spirit
  even when we aren't so sure we like what we
    have won.
  And help us to be true to your calling
  even when we aren't so sure we want to follow
    in your way.
Amen.

Seventh Sunday of Easter

24 May 1998
27 May 2001
23 May 2004

𝒜lpha and
Omega

Scripture

- *Acts 7:55–60.* Stephen is stoned to death, the first Christian martyr.
- *Revelation 22:12–14,16–17,20.* The Alpha and Omega, first and last, beginning and end
- *John 17:20–26.* Jesus prays that his followers may be united with him and the Creator.

Theme

Before his death, Jesus prayed for unity among his followers—unity that reflected the oneness of himself with the One who sent him. He knew the road ahead would not be easy for himself or for his followers. Stephen was the first of many of Jesus' followers to be killed for believing in him. Jesus, along with the One who sent him, is truly Alpha and Omega, the first and last. The struggle of the story makes sense when you know how it begins and ends.

Focusing Object
The Greek letters *alpha* (A) and *omega* (Ω) on a cloth, a candle, or written on a piece of paper

Reflections

For Adults

Our faith tells us that God was there at the beginning of the world, and God will be there at the end of the world. Our faith tells us that God was there at the beginning of our life, and God will be there when our life ends.

- Does understanding the Alpha and Omega of the world and of our life help us in our daily struggles and sufferings? Why or why not?
- When you think of the end of the world, what are your concerns? Do you think you will be alive to see it? Why or why not? Where does your faith fit into this picture?
- When you think about the end of your life, what are your concerns? What would worry or frighten you the most? What would comfort or assure you? Where does your faith fit into this picture?

For Teenagers

- What struggles in your life today were not present when you were a small child? Are you happier now than you were then, or do you think you were happier when you were a child? Do you think you will be happier as an adult than you are now? Why or why not?
- God was with you when your life began. God will be there when your life ends. Does knowing that God is there in the beginning and the end change your life at all? Does it affect the way you look at your struggles? How and why? Or why not?
- The Book of Revelation tells us that Jesus is returning soon. How soon is soon? What do you think? Is it important to know? Why or why not? Would life be different if you thought it would be over in a day or a week or a month or a year? How would you do things differently? Give some examples.

For Children

- What is the beginning of the day like for you? What do you do when you first get up? What is your favorite thing to do in the morning?
- What is the end of the day like for you? What do you do when it is time to get ready for bed? What is your favorite thing to do at night?
- Jesus wants us to know that he is with us at every beginning and at every ending. He is

there every morning and every night. Does it help you to know that Jesus is always there with you? How does knowing about Jesus make life better?

Closing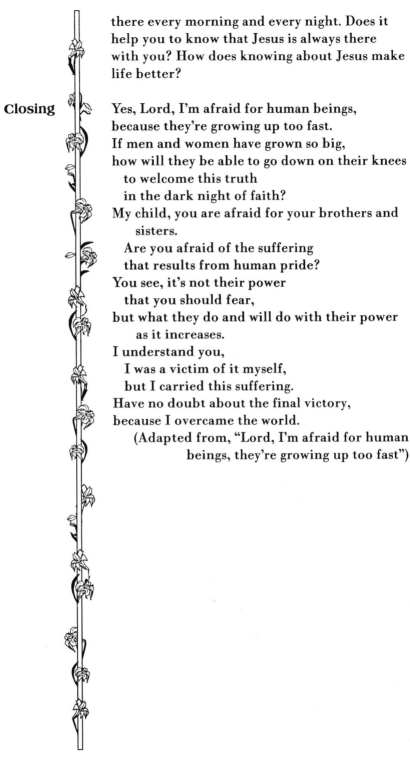

Yes, Lord, I'm afraid for human beings,
because they're growing up too fast.
If men and women have grown so big,
how will they be able to go down on their knees
   to welcome this truth
   in the dark night of faith?
My child, you are afraid for your brothers and
   sisters.
   Are you afraid of the suffering
   that results from human pride?
You see, it's not their power
   that you should fear,
but what they do and will do with their power
   as it increases.
I understand you,
   I was a victim of it myself,
   but I carried this suffering.
Have no doubt about the final victory,
because I overcame the world.
   (Adapted from, "Lord, I'm afraid for human
           beings, they're growing up too fast")

Pentecost Sunday

26 May 1996
18 May 1997
31 May 1998
23 May 1999
11 June 2000
3 June 2001
19 May 2002
8 June 2003

Winds of the Spirit

Scripture

○ *Acts 2:1–11.* A rush of wind, tongues of fire, and people speaking different languages
• *1 Corinthians 12:3–7,12–13.* Different gifts, but the same Spirit; many members, but one body
• *John 20:19–23.* Peace be with you. Receive the Holy Spirit.

Theme

Pentecost Sunday is called the birthday of the church. This day celebrates the Holy Spirit coming to the followers of Jesus in a rush of wind and tongues of fire. The Spirit gave them the gifts they needed to go forth and be church. These gifts vary—they are as different as we are. But we are all needed, and we are all members of one united body.

Focusing Object
A wind catcher, wind chimes, or windmill

Reflections

For Adults

• The disciples, previously frightened, confused, and doubtful, became suddenly charged with courage and knowledge and commitment when the wind roared, the fire appeared, and the Spirit came. When have you been afraid, confused, and doubtful? How did you regain your courage, understanding, and commitment?

194

- Often it is said that the winds of the Spirit blow where they will blow, and their blowing can bring unexpected changes. What part did the Holy Spirit play in your change of heart? Was it a change of your spirit as well? Was it unexpected?
- Pentecost is called the birthday of the church because that is when the followers of Jesus actually became church. What does it mean to be church? What gifts does it take? What gifts do you have that you can offer?

For Teenagers

Pentecost is called the birthday of the church because before Pentecost, there really was no church. Jesus had ascended back into the heavens, the Apostles were hanging around, scared and confused, and nobody knew what to do. Going out to baptize people and preach about Jesus was the last thing they had in mind because their lives would be in danger.

But Pentecost celebrates the coming of the Holy Spirit—the force that turned a bunch of frightened, mixed-up folks into church. There was a rush of wind, tongues of fire, and then suddenly there was courage, knowledge, direction, and commitment! Everyone started speaking and was understood, no matter what the language of the listener was! These were saints suddenly on fire with the Holy Spirit. And it all began with the wind and fire of the Spirit.

- What changes in you do you wish the Spirit could blow your way? How can you cooperate with the Spirit? In what ways do you need more courage, knowledge, direction, or commitment? What else might you need?
- In what ways are you and your parish like the disciples before Pentecost? In what ways are you and your parish like the disciples after Pentecost?
- When people speak about your school, would they say that it has school spirit? What do they mean by that? How is school spirit like the Holy Spirit?

- When it is really windy, your hair blows all around, your clothes whip, and leaves and dust blow wildly. What do you like about the wind? What don't you like about the wind?

The Holy Spirit is like the wind. When the wind blows in, things change; rain comes, or cold weather comes, or snow comes, or sometimes a tornado comes. When the Holy Spirit blows in, people change. The Holy Spirit can make people brave, smart, or excited about God.

- Have you ever felt brave, smart, or excited about God? What happened? Do you think the Holy Spirit helped to blow those feelings over you?

After Jesus ascended to heaven, his friends were feeling confused and afraid. The first time the Holy Spirit blew in those feelings of being smart, brave, and excited about God was the day we call Pentecost. The Spirit blew those feelings into Jesus' followers, and that was the first day of the church. We call it the birthday of the church.

- What is your idea of the perfect birthday party? How can we have a birthday party for the church?

Closing

Dear Heart of the Eternal Rose—
O Many-colored Heart of Fire—
That in our Lord's green garden grows,
Come, Holy Spirit, come inspire!

O Wind, down heaven's long lanes blow,
Warm, perfume-laden Breath of Love,
O Sweetness, on our hearts bestow,
Your holy blessing from above.

O Holy wind! O Breath! O Fire!
Come, Holy Spirit, come inspire!

(Adapted from "Pentecost")

Index by Theme

Theme	Scripture	Pages
Jesus' Passion:		
Crucifixion	Mark 14:1—15:47	130–132
Jesus forgives cruci- fiers	Luke 22:14—23:56	133–135
Peter denies Jesus	Matthew 26:14—27:66	126–129
Jesus teaches:		
Grain dies to produce fruit	John 12:20–33	120–122
I am the Good Shepherd	John 10:11–18	161–163
I am vine, you are branches	John 15:1–8	170–172
I came that they may have life	John 10:1–10	158–160
Love each other, Spirit will come	John 14:15–21	176–178
One without sin cast first stone	John 8:1–11	123–125
The Prodigal	Luke 15:1–3,11–32	114–116
Mary:		
Angel Gabriel comes to Mary	Luke 1:26–38	47–49
Mary reflects upon events	Luke 2:16–21	67–69
Mary visits Elizabeth	Luke 1:39–45	50–52

Theme	Scripture	Pages
Virtues:		
Comfort		
Comfort my people	Isaiah 40:1–5,9–11	29–31
God wipes away all tears	Revelation 7:9, 14–17	164–166
Faith		
Write down what you see	Revelation 1:9–19	147–149
Glory		
Alpha and Omega	Revelation 22:12–14, 16–17,20	191–193
God is all the light we need	Revelation 21:10–14, 22–23	183–185
Gratitude		
Thankful for part- nership	Philippians 1:4–6, 8–11	32–34
Hope		
Branch will spring forth	Jeremiah 33:14–16	23–25
New heaven, new earth	Revelation 21:1–5	173–175
Humility		
Unworthy to tie Jesus' sandal	Luke 3:10–18	41–43
Justice		
Good news to the oppressed	Isaiah 61:1–2,10–11	38–40

Theme	Scripture	Pages
Patience		
Planting seeds; waiting	James 5:7–10	35–37
Peace		
Lion and lamb together	Isaiah 11:1–10	26–28
Swords into plow-shares	Isaiah 2:1–5	17–19
Self-Esteem		
We are God's handi-work	Ephesians 2:4–10	111–113
Surrender		
God as potter, we as clay	Isaiah 63:16–17; 64:1–8	20–22
Trust		
Believers are chil-dren of God	1 John 5:1–6	145–146

Index by Focusing Object

Acknowledgments *(continued)*

The excerpts on pages 19, 43, 122, 144, 154, 169, and 187 are from *One Hundred Graces*, selected by Marcia and Jack Kelly (New York: Bell Tower/Harmony Books, 1992), pages 94, 79, 97, 53, 16, 50, and 47, respectively. Copyright © 1992 by Marcia and Jack Kelly.

The excerpts on pages 22, 37, 95, 107, 119, and 149 are from *Prayers for a Planetary Pilgrim*, by Edward M. Hays (Leavenworth, KS: Forest of Peace Publishing, 1988), pages 195, 129, 99, 214, 199, and 216, respectively. Copyright by Forest of Peace Publishing. Reprinted by permission of Forest of Peace Publishing, 251 Muncie Road, Leavenworth, KS 66048-4946.

The poems on pages 28 and 81–82 are by Don Larmore, Blessed Sacrament Church, 518 State, Grand Island, NE 68801. Reprinted with permission.

The excerpt on page 31 by Sally Latkovich appeared in *One Hundred Graces* (New York: Bell Tower/Harmony Books, 1992), page 28. Copyright by Sally Latkovich. Used by permission of the author.

The excerpt on page 34 by Muriel Lester appeared on a Fellowship of Reconciliation bookmark, Box 271, Nyack, NY 10960. Used by permission of the Fellowship of Reconciliation.

The excerpt on page 40 is from *American Indian Prayers and Poetry*, edited by J. Ed Sharpe (Cherokee, NC: Cherokee Publishing, 1985), page 4. Used with permission.

The excerpts on pages 52, 104, 110, and 141 are from *Prayers for the Domestic Church*, by Edward M. Hays (Easton, KS: Shantivanam House of Prayer, 1979), pages 31, 50, 43, and 94, respectively. Copyright by Forest of Peace Publishing. Reprinted by permission of Forest of Peace Publishing, 251 Muncie Road, Leavenworth, KS 66048-4946.

"One of the unique characteristics of this book, along with reflections on the lectionary readings, is the inclusion of a focusing object. Besides lending insights into the Scriptures, the focusing object trains people to see symbolically. In doing so, it enhances the ability 'to see more than meets the eye,' to see the extraordinary in the ordinary, the sacred in the secular." **Dr. Maureen Gallagher,** Archbishop's Delegate for Parishes, Diocese of Milwaukee, Wisconsin

"Lisa-Marie is definitely 'in touch' with the needs of young people and families—and how they approach the Word of God. *In Touch with the Word* will not only help various generations in praying the Scriptures, but will also assist homilists in making the Word come alive in their preaching." **Thomas N. Tomaszek, MEd, MTS,** Director, Spectrum Resources, Milwaukee, Wisconsin, and consultant to the National Federation for Catholic Youth Ministry's Prayer and Worship Project Team